C.A.I.R. IS HAMAS

HOW THE FEDERAL GOVERNMENT PROVED THAT THE COUNCIL ON AMERICAN-ISLAMIC RELATIONS IS A FRONT FOR TERRORISM

For more information about this book, visit
SECUREFREEDOM.ORG

C.A.I.R. is Hamas is published in the United States by the
Center for Security Policy Press,
a division of the Center for Security Policy.

ISBN-13: 978-1540707550
ISBN-10: 1540707555

The Center for Security Policy
1901 Pennsylvania Avenue, NW, Suite 201
Washington, D.C. 20006
Phone: 202-835-9077
Email: info@SecureFreedom.org
For more information, visit SecureFreedom.org

Book design by Bravura Books
Cover design by J.P. Zarruk

Contents

INTRODUCTION

I n 2008, the United States Department of Justice successfully prosecuted the Holy Land Foundation for Relief and Development (HLF) and its founders on 108 charges, including material support for terrorism, money laundering and tax fraud. The government's theory of the case, successfully proven at trial, was that the Holy Land Foundation was established as a front group of the Palestine Committee—a covert organization of the U.S. branch of the Muslim Brotherhood—and that its purpose in this conspiracy was to provide funds for the Palestinian terrorist organization, Hamas.

In order to prove its case, the U.S. Government successfully demonstrated, first, that the Muslim Brotherhood was an international organization operating across the globe, including in the United States. During the launch of the First Intifada against Israel in the early 1980s, the Muslim Brotherhood decided to establish "Palestine Committees" across the globe in order to provide support for its then-new organization, Hamas, which was engaged in a war of terrorism against the state of Israel and its civilian population. The job of the Palestine Committees was, in their own words, "to make the Palestinian cause victorious and to support it with what it needs of media, money, men and all of that."[1]

One of the key elements of the prosecution's case was audio surveillance of a meeting held over the course of two days at a Courtyard by Marriot hotel in Philadelphia, Pennsylvania, in October 1993—one year prior to the designation of Hamas as a terrorist organization by the Clinton Administration.

The successful surveillance of the 1993 "Philly Meeting," as it came to be called, was vital to the U.S. Government's efforts to demonstrate the role of U.S.-based Muslim Brotherhood organizations in supporting Hamas. It also became a window into the operations of the Brotherhood in the United States at a time where preparations were being made for the designation of Hamas as a terrorist group, the first serious threat to the Brotherhood's operations since it began in the early 1960s.

In particular, the Philly Meeting stands out as the earliest record of the founding of the Council on American Islamic Relations (CAIR) as an organization both created under the auspices of the Palestine Committee and in the context of its goal, support for Hamas. In that framework, CAIR had a responsibility for providing media support and propaganda on behalf of the Muslim Brotherhood and Hamas. The founding of CAIR would represent a new era, as the Brotherhood began to take its message not just to the Palestinian and Muslim communities in America, but also to the American people more broadly.

CAIR's founding was an important event because this new front of the Palestine Committee would be empowered not just to dissimulate and propagandize on

1

behalf of Hamas, but for the larger Muslim Brotherhood cause as a whole. As such, the proposal to create this new organization—first broached at the 1993 Philly Meeting—required and received the approval of the Global Muslim Brotherhood leadership itself, according to information obtained by the FBI.[2]

As the Palestine Committee, including CAIR, prepared to operate in a new and potentially hostile American environment—where open reference to support for jihad against Israel and financial support for Hamas would no longer be legally tolerated—they would be guided by the words spoken by CAIR founder Omar Ahmad, who was present at the meeting. Ahmad noted the importance of misleading Americans about the true nature of the Muslim Brotherhood and its support for the terror war against Israel.

"I believe that our problem is that we stopped working underground. We will recognize the source of any message that comes out of us. I mean, if a message is publicized, we will know...," Omar Ahmad told the Philly meeting participants, "the media person among us will recognize that you send two messages; one to the Americans and one to the Muslims. "[3]

Echoes of Omar Ahmad's words remain visible today. CAIR, the last remaining organization of the original Palestine Committee, continues to operate in much the same manner as it was originally envisioned in Philadelphia. Portraying itself as a "Muslim civil rights group," CAIR continues to enjoy lobbying access to state and federal legislators, high-level meetings with members of the executive branch, and the support and endorsement of uncurious media outlets.

CAIR cloaks itself in claims of moderation while promoting the same Islamic supremacist agenda of encouraging American Muslims to support Jihad, both against Israel and elsewhere. While the group publicly promotes a toned-down version of Islamist rhetoric for the American public as a whole, its own history belies these claims of moderation.

A number of CAIR's employees and board members have been indicted, convicted and deported for terrorism or material support for terrorism, as noted by the Louisiana State House of Representatives when it voted to support a prohibition against state officials "interacting with the group.[4]

Contained in this volume are annotated excerpts of court transcripts from *U.S. v Holy Land Foundation for Relief & Development*, as FBI Agent Lara Burns walks Acting U.S. District Attorney Barry Jonas through the events leading up to the Philly Meeting in October 1993, followed by the meeting itself. These transcripts offer a valuable window into the deliberations and operations of the Muslim Brotherhood in America.

Wherever possible, the text of Burn's testimony has been left as it appears from court records. In instances where we have made the decision to excerpt portions of testimony, ellipses have been used. Every effort has been made to excerpt from the transcript only in order to streamline the often unwieldy back and forth of a court setting, with great care taken not to distort the context or full meaning of the included segments.

Annotations are written in italics. In cases where Agent Burns refers to a document, or to the transcript of an FBI wiretap or audio surveillance, the relevant excerpt of the document or text is included in cases where we believe it would prove beneficial to the reader.

We have also included, as appendices, brief summaries and excerpts from the Philly Meeting that are informative – particularly, in regards to the formation or nature of CAIR – but were not invoked during this section of courtroom testimony, which (naturally) focused on the defendants at trial in the case, rather than on the principals involved in CAIR's founding.

It is our hope that this annotated transcript, with assembled appendices, will be a useful tool for those looking to educate themselves about the Holy Land Foundation trial, the window it opened into the reality of Muslim Brotherhood operations in the United States, and the ominous genesis and true nature of the organization known as CAIR. We believe it serves as a worthy addition to the Center for Security Policy's "Archival Series" of published Muslim Brotherhood documents.

TESTIMONY

Excerpts of Lara Burns, FBI Agent, testifying for the U.S. Government in U.S. v. Holy Land Foundation for Relief and Development, et al.

THE COURT: Mr. Jonas?

MR. JONAS: Thank you, sir.

Q. (BY MR. JONAS) Agent Burns, I want to get back and talk about the Palestine Committee.

A. Okay.

Q. Did the Palestine Committee have any meetings that were recorded by the FBI?

A. Yes.

Q. And is there one in particular that stands out in your mind?

A. There is.

Q. When did that meeting occur?

A. October 2nd and 3rd of 1993.

Q. I am sorry. Could you repeat that?

A. October 2nd and 3rd of 1993.

Q. Where did it take place?

A. At a Courtyard by Marriott in Philadelphia, Pennsylvania.

Q. With regard to the Israeli-Palestinian issues, what was going on at that time?

A. The Oslo Peace Accords had just been signed.

Q. Did the FBI record this entire meeting?

A. They did.

Q. And was the recording transcribed into a transcript?

A. Yes. A majority of the conversation was in Arabic, and there were English transcriptions of the conversations, and I have reviewed those.

Q. Okay. Generally speaking, what was the purpose of the meeting?

A. The purpose of the meeting was for the Palestinian Committee members to discuss how they were going to continue to operate in the United States in light of the signing of the peace accords between the Palestinians and the Israelis.

Q. Okay. For purposes of your testimony, would it be fair to call this the Philadelphia meeting or the Philly meeting?

A. Yes.

Q. Were there planning conversations on the call – Withdrawn. Did any of the Defendants or any of the participants have any phone calls where they discussed the planning of the Philadelphia meeting?

A. Yes.

Q. And were those phone calls intercepted by the FBI?

A. Some of them were, yes.

Q. Do you have what has been marked Ashqar Wiretap No. 1?

A. I do.

Q. And can you remind us who Ashqar is?

A. Ashqar is one of the members of the Palestinian Committee that we saw on the list. Also his home is the one that was searched in that covert search in December of '93.

> Abdel Haleem Ashqar was a Palestine Committee member and one of the founders of the Al Aqsa Educational Fund, an organization suspected of helping to finance Hamas. He would be acquitted of terrorism finance charges, in part because some of the evidence against him predated Hamas' designation as a terrorist organization. Ashqar would later be convicted and sentenced to 11 years in prison on charges of contempt and obstruction of justice for refusing to testify in a grand jury hearing about Hamas finance activities in the United States.[5]

Q. With regard to Ashqar Wiretap No. 1, who are the participants in this call?

A. Abdel Haleem Ashqar, the Defendant Shukri Abu Baker, and Omar Yehia, also known as Omar Ahmad.

Q. What is the date of the call?

A. September 13th, 1993.

MR. JONAS: Your Honor, at this time I would offer into evidence Ashqar Wiretap No. 1 and 1-A.

THE COURT: That is admitted.

(BY MR. JONAS) And again, Agent Burns, is this the whole call that we have, or are we offering into evidence a redacted version?

6

A. We are offering portions of the call.

Q. All right.

MR. JONAS: If we can play the portions that we have, please.

(Whereupon, Ashqar Wiretap No. 1 was played while questions were propounded.)

...

Q. (BY MR. JONAS) Agent Burns, who is OM?

A. That is Omar Ahmad.

> *Omar Ahmad aka Omar Yehia, was one of the founding members of CAIR and president of the Islamic Association of Palestine[6] (about which more will be said later). Ahmad's role as President Emeritus of CAIR was one of the reasons cited by the FBI for their policy of cutting ties to CAIR.[7] In the aftermath of the HLF trial, during a deposition for the successful deportation of CAIR Board member Nabil Sadoun[8], an FBI agent would describe Ahmad's presence at the 1993 Philly meeting and identify Ahmad as "one of the leaders of HAMAS."[9]*

Q. And who is SH?

A. The Defendant Shukri Abu Baker.

> *Shukri Abu Baker was one of the founders of the Holy Land Foundation, and one of the defendants in the case. A resident of Garland, Texas, at the conclusion of the Holy Land Foundation trial Abu Baker would be sentenced to 65 years in prison for: "10 counts of conspiracy to provide, and the provision of, material support to a designated foreign terrorist organization; 11 counts of conspiracy to provide, and the provision of, funds, goods and services to a Specially Designated Terrorist; 10 counts of conspiracy to commit, and the commission of, money laundering; one count of conspiracy to impede and impair the Internal Revenue Service (IRS); and one count of filing a false tax return."[10]*

Q. It said a moment ago Association and Fund. Where have we seen those names?

A. The Association is the IAP, and the Fund is the Occupied Land Fund or the Holy Land Foundation.

THE COURT: I don't know that the jury remembers always what these acronyms are.

THE WITNESS: The Islamic Association for Palestine, the IAP.

> *The Islamic Association of Palestine (IAP) was an organization that the Government described as the "Propaganda and information" arm of the Palestine Committee that received money from Hamas leader Mousa Abu Marzook to provide Hamas propaganda in the United States.[11] The government brief goes on to describe their case against IAP as follows:*

> The IAP, which involved the defendant Ghassan Elashi as an original incorporator and bank account signatory, was designed as a propaganda facility, responsible for Intifada festivals (involving the defendant HLF), pro-Hamas publications, and the general rallying of support within the American Palestinian community. The IAP was the first organization to publish an English version of the Hamas charter, which as previously explained vows to replace Israel, the West Bank, and Gaza with an Islamic state.

> CAIR's founders Nihad Awad, Omar Ahmad, and Rafiq Jaber were all members of the Islamic Association of Palestine (IAP).[12]

Q. (BY MR. JONAS) And where have we seen the IAP and the HLF together?

A. Organizations that were part of the Palestine Committee.

Q. Do you see where Omar mentions Abu Ibrahim?

A. Yes.

Q. Who is that?

A. That is the Defendant Mohamed El Mezain.

> Mohamed El Mezain, Chairman of the Holy Land Foundation, was sentenced to 15 years in prison for "one count of conspiracy to provide material support to a designated foreign terrorist organization." El Mezain was the founder of the Islamic Center of Passaic County, New Jersey, and bragged that the mosque provided $1.8 Million for Hamas activities.[13]

...

Q. Agent Burns, there is a discussion of papers and writing. From your review of the Philadelphia transcript, were papers presented to the participants?

A. Yes, they were.

Q. And what does that mean?

A. Well, the Philadelphia meeting was separated into sessions based on topics, and individuals wrote papers regarding certain topics, like media and charity work, and presented those papers to the meeting attendees and they discussed the papers.

...

Q. Agent Burns, was there another call where there was a discussion about the meeting prior to the meeting taking place?

A. There was.

Q. Do you have before you Ashqar Wiretap No. 2?

A. I do.

Q. Who are the participants in this call?

A. Abdel Haleem Ashqar and Omar Yehia, also known as Omar Ahmad.

Q. What is the date of this call?

A. This one is dated September 27th, 1993.

MR. JONAS: Your Honor, at this time I would offer into evidence Ashqar Wiretap No. 2.

THE COURT: That is admitted.

MR. JONAS: I don't think we are going to play this one. I think we are just going to read the first page.

Q. (BY MR. JONAS) Agent Burns, do you have that in front of you?

A. I do.

THE COURT: Do you also want to offer 2-A?

MR. JONAS: Yes, Your Honor. Thank you for reminding me. No. 2-A.

THE COURT: Those are admitted.

MR. JONAS: Thank you, sir.

MR. JONAS: Page 2.

Q. (BY MR. JONAS) Agent Burns, if you can just read this first page, and I will let you know when to stop.

MR. DRATEL: Can we get a date of the conversation?

Q. (BY MR. JONAS) Agent Burns do you know the date of the call?

A. Yes. It is September 27, 1993.

Q. Do you see where the date is on the transcript?

A. That is correct.

Q. Okay. If you can read the first page or the second page of the transcript, the first page where there is actually conversation, and I will let you know when to stop.

A. Okay. The first speaker AB is Ashqar, and he says, "By God, no. I mean, nothing. May God protect you. Everything is fine. Nothing new. May God bless you." Abou Mohamed Isam is coming." "Who?" "Isam." "Okay, good God willing." "I am just waiting for what's his name, Riyad, to send me a reply about the other three, who are Yousif, Salah, and Al Hanooti." "Oh, has not Salah answered you yet?" "By God, my brother, I – I couldn't get ahold of him. So, God willing, I will catch him tomorrow, I mean. I didn't find him yesterday. And I contracted him a while ago, but nobody answers, I mean, so – " "Good." "Good. But I don't know – " "Now, it will become how many, six people, I mean, will come." "Hmm. What's his name, Al Hanooti, Salah as well, Riyad, Abou Ibrahim, and Isam. That makes it six, I mean". "Jawad." "No. I meant from New Jersey. Six, I mean." "Abou Ibrahim, Riyad, and Isam. Those three are for sure." –

Al Hanooti refers to Mohammed Al Hanooti. Al Hanooti served as president of the Islamic Association for Palestine, and was suspected by the U.S. Government of raising up to $6 million for Hamas. In addition to attending the Philly Meeting and being named an unindicted co-conspirator in the Holy Land Foundation Trial, Hanooti was also an unindicted co-conspirator in the 1993 World Trade Center Bombing and helped to raise funds for the legal defense of Hamas leader Mousa Abu Marzook. Hanooti would serve as a leader of the Muslim Brotherhood's organization for Islamic jurisprudence in the United States, the Fiqh Council of North America (FCNA) and as Imam of the Dar Al-Hijrah Mosque in Falls Church Virginia, a mosque linked to AL Qaeda ideologue Anwar Awlaki, as well as multiple other terror investigations. Hanooti passed away in 2015.[14]

Q. Agent Burns, you can stop there. And Abou Ibrahim is?

A. The defendant Mohamed El Mezain.

Q. And where was he living at the time this call took place?

A. In New Jersey.

Q. Looking at the rest of this transcript, generally what do they talk about?

A. Who will be attending the Philadelphia meeting.

Q. Is this really following on the heels of the last call that we played?

A. It does.

Q. Agent Burns, in the course of the material that you reviewed, did you come across any written itinerary for the Philadelphia meeting?

A. I did.

Q. Do you have before you Ashqar Search No. 4?

A. I do.

Q. Where did that document come from?

A. That came from the covert search of the home of Abdel Haleem Ashqar.

Q. And Ashqar was a participant in that first call we just played planning the meeting?

A. In both of the calls that we just discussed.

MR. JONAS: Your Honor, at this time I would offer into evidence Ashqar Search No. 4.

THE COURT: That is admitted.

MR. JONAS: If we can put that on the screen, please, starting with the first page. The next page.

Q. (BY MR. JONAS) Agent Burns, the first page it said – Withdrawn. What language is this document in?

A. Arabic.

MR. JONAS: And if we can go to page 4, please.

Q. (BY MR. JONAS) What is the title of this document?

A. "Future of Islamic Action for Palestine in North America seminar, 2-3 October, 1993."

Q. The title "Islamic Action for Palestine," have we seen that title used in any of the documents you testified about already?

A. Yes. I believe it has been in several, most prominently in the October 1992 internal memorandum from the international Muslim Brotherhood.

Q. That was one of the Elbarasse documents you testified about?

A. That is correct.

> The Elbarasse documents refers to a cache of documents seized at the home of Muslim Brotherhood Palestine Committee member Ismail Elbarasse. Elbarasse's home was searched after he and his wife were caught filming the structural supports of the Chesapeake Bay Bridge by an alert law enforcement officer. Included as evidence for the search warrant was Elbarasse's attendance at the "Philly Meeting".[15] The subsequent search of the Annandale, Virginia property would uncover a large archive of Muslim Brotherhood internal documents, speeches, audiotapes and other materials. In all, forty separate documents from the search were submitted as evidence by the prosecution in the Holy Land Foundation Trial.

Q. On this particular document, just summarize it for us so we don't need to read the whole thing.

A. Basically it lists under No. 1 the goals of the seminar, the Philadelphia meeting. No. 2, describes how the sessions will be moderated and lists the names of like, for example, session moderator under the first session, if you will scroll down, is the Defendant Shukri Abu Baker. So it identifies the topic of the first session, the people who will participate, the individual who is moderating.

And the same thing for the second session, which is charity work, and identifies who will present the papers, and who will be moderating the session. And on the next page it identifies the topic of the third session, and who would be presenting papers, and the moderator of the session.

Q. Thank you. Agent Burns, did you create a summary chart identifying who attended the session and the documents that you reviewed that helped you identify those people?

A. Yes.

Q. What did you base your summary chart on?

A. We based the summary chart on a variety of different exhibits – the planning phone calls that we just listened to, the actual meeting transcripts themselves, and in the transcripts we were able to identify some of the speakers at the conference. There were also records from the search warrant indicating – like American Express bills indicating plane tickets that were purchased for individuals. In addition, there were records obtained from the Marriott Hotel at the time the meeting took place.

Q. What Marriott?

A. I believe it was Courtyard by Marriott in Philadelphia.

MR. JONAS: Your Honor, may I approach?

THE COURT: Yes.

Q. (BY MR. JONAS) Agent Burns, I am holding up for you what has been marked as Philly Meeting Summary. Is this the chart that you prepared based upon the records you talked about of who attended the Philadelphia meeting?

A. Yes, we prepared that.

Q. Would this aid the jury in your testimony this afternoon?

A. Yes.

PHILADELPHIA MEETING October 2-3, 1993

Attendees	Organizations	HLF AMEX Records-Flights (exh: Amer1, Amer2)	Marriott Hotel Records (exh: Marriott)	Speaker at Conference (exh: Philly Meeting 1-18)	Surveillance Photos (exh: Philly Pictures 1-6)	Planning Phone Calls (exh: Ashqar Wire Tap 1-5)
Shukri Abu Baker	PC, HLF, IAP	√	√	√	√	√
Ghassan Elashi	PC, HLF, IAP	√	√	√	√	
Mufid Abdulqader	HLF, Al Sakra Band					
Haitham Maghawri	HLF	√	√	√	√	
Akram Kharoubi	PC, HLF, IAP	√	√	√	√	
Omar Ahmad	PC, IAP	√	√	√		
Ismail Elbarasse	PC, IAP		√			√
Abdel Haleem Ashqar	PC, AEF	√	√	√	√	√
Ghassan Saleh Dahduli	PC, IAP	√	√	√	√	√
Muin Shabib	PC	√	√	√		√
Abdul Rahman Barakji	IAP	√				
Sharif Battikhi	HLF	√				
Riad Ahmed			√			
Hassan Sabri	IAP		√	√		√
Abdul Jabar Hamdan	HLF		√	√		√
Ayman Sharawi	PC					
Jawad al Hamad	Palestine Section		√	√		√
Abdel Salam				√		√
Nihad Awad	PC, CAIR			√		√
Osama	IAP			√		
Abu Ahmad				√		√
Mohamed El-Mezain	PC, HLF					√
Mohamed Al Hanooti	PC		√			√
Salah						√
Issam Siraj	PC					√
Yasser Bushnaq	PC, IAP					√
Mohamed Abbas	PC					√

13

MR. JONAS: Your Honor, at this time I would offer into evidence Philly Meeting Summary.

THE COURT: That is admitted.

...

Q. Okay. Can you first walk us through this by explaining across the top what the row is?

A. Well, the first column would be the attendees, the name of the individual that we will be discussing. The next column are the organizations that the individual belonged to according to the evidence that we have discussed. The next column is a column which references AMEX No. 1, which is an exhibit that we will be discussing here. If that individual appeared in those records as having attended the Philadelphia meeting, there will be a checkmark by that individual's name under that column. The next column is Marriott Hotel records, which were the records that were obtained from the Marriott Hotel at the time of the conference. If the individual Defendant's name appears in those records, a checkmark will appear across from his name under that column. The next column is listed "speaker at conference," and we have 18 transcripts of conversations that took place during the conference that were recorded. If the individual either self-identified or his voice was identified by the language specialist as speaking at the conference, there will be a checkmark under his name on the chart. Next, there were some surveillance photos that were taken by FBI agents back in 1993 of the meeting, and if individuals could be positively identified in any of the surveillance photos, there is a check under that column by their name. And then finally, the last column is for planning phone calls, and if the individuals were mentioned as being invited to attend the conference in those calls, there will be a checkmark by that individual's name under that column.

MR. JONAS: Your Honor, at this time I would like to offer into evidence the supporting documentation for this chart, to the extent some of it is not already admitted. We have AMEX No. 1.

Q. (BY MR. JONAS) And Agent Burns, whose records are AMEX No. 1?

A. AMEX No. 1 are records obtained from the – I am looking to make sure I am right, because we had American Express records from two different places. From American Express.

Q. Whose American Express records are they?

A. The Holy Land Foundation.

Q. Okay.MR. JONAS: Your Honor, we also offer to admit Marriott.

Q. (BY MR. JONAS) What is Marriott? What exhibit is that?

A. Marriott is the name of the exhibit for the Marriott Hotel records.

MR. JONAS: We offer to admit Philly Meeting No. 1 through 18.

Q. (BY MR. JONAS) And what is that?

A. Those are the English transcriptions of the conversations at the meeting.

MR. JONAS: Your Honor, I will have to explain in a moment what we did with those.

Q. (BY MR. JONAS) And finally Philly Pictures 1 through 6?

A. Those were some of the surveillance photos that agents took back then.

Q. Okay.

MR. JONAS: Your Honor, with Philly Meeting No. 1 through 18, which are the transcripts of this meeting that took place, we are offering it a little bit differently than the intercepted calls. We are offering the whole conference into evidence. And I will have Agent Burns explain in a moment why it is divided into 18. So the audio disk, which would be Philly Meeting No. 1-A is a disk of that whole tape for that section. But in addition, we are offering an excerpted transcript. So we have the full transcript and then an excerpted transcript, and that is Philly Meeting E. So if we have for example, No. 1 would be the full transcript, 1-A is the audio, and 1-E is the excerpt of that particular session of Philly.

THE COURT: You are offering No. 1, 1-A and 1-E.

MR. JONAS: Yes, sir, through No. 18, 18-A, and 18-E.

MS. HOLLANDER: I just have a question. We don't have any objection to these, but is that the entire Philly meeting?

MR. JONAS: No. 1 through 18 is the entire Philly meeting.

MS. HOLLANDER: Okay. We don't object, as long as it is the entire meeting.

MR. JONAS: That is my understanding.

THE COURT: And the AMEX records is AMEX No. 1?

MR. JONAS: Yes, sir.

MS. HOLLANDER: We don't object to the others.

THE COURT: All right. Those are admitted, then.

Q. (BY MR. JONAS) Agent Burns, first of all, why is there 18 tapes or transcripts of the Philadelphia meeting?

A. As I understand it, back in 1993 the equipment that the FBI used to record these conversations, it was some type of tape. I don't know if it was a cassette tape, or I believe it may have actually been one of those old reel to reels. But they were limited in length, so that once one was filled up they would have to remove it and replace it with a new tape. So we have a transcript for each tape that was made. So there were approximately 18 tape recordings of that meeting.

Q. And did the FBI record this meeting pursuant to a court order?

A. They did.

Q. Was this part of the intelligence investigations of certain individuals?

A. It was the intelligence investigation of Ashqar.

...

MR. JONAS: If we can pull up AMEX 1, page 6, please. Your Honor, I assume, just for the record, they are all admitted, the documents I offered into evidence?

THE COURT: Yes.

MR. JONAS: Thank you, sir.

Q. (BY MR. JONAS) Agent Burns, do you see any individuals who went to the Philadelphia conference on this page with particular charges?

A. Yes. I am going to look at my hard copy because it is a little bit difficult to read on my screen.

...

MR. JONAS: Page 12, please.

THE WITNESS: I guess the entire middle section you can highlight. This shows that on September 16th up in the upper left corner, September 16, 1993, that the Holy Land Foundation purchased an airline ticket for G. Saleh, who is Ghassan Saleh, from Dallas to Philadelphia. Moving across the page, on September 17th, 1993, the Holy Land Foundation purchased an airline ticket for O. Amhad[sic] to Philadelphia, which would be Omar Ahmad.

244   0244/0265

ITEM 10 $55.85
TIGER SOFTWARE INC   CORAL GABLES   FL

Cardmember Account No.	Date of Charge	Reference Code	Approval Code
3783-647338-93038	09/20/93	692669001	

Service Establishment and Location
TIGER SOFTWARE INC   CORAL GABLES   FL

Record of Charge

COMPUTER SOFTWARE

ROC NUMBER 5828550010

S/E #   4095879403

TOTAL CHARGE AMOUNT   **$55.85**

ITEM 11 $319.00
Q PLUS E SOFTWARE   RALEIGH   NC

Cardmember Account No.	Date of Charge	Reference Code	Approval Date
3783-647338-93038	09/20/93	003720083	

Service Establishment and Location
Q PLUS E SOFTWARE   RALEIGH   NC

Record of Charge

COMPUTERS/SFTWRE/HRDWRE

ROC NUMBER   03720083

S/E #   4328703027

TOTAL INVOICE AMOUNT   **$319.00**

ITEM 12 $350.00
AMERICAN AIRLINES   AUSTIN   TX

Cardmember Account No.	Transaction Date	Ticket Number
3783-647338-93038	09/16/93	0011350611A164

Passenger Name   Ticketing Airline
SALEH/S   AMERICAN AIRLINES

Travel Agency Name   Issue Address
TRAVELSCOPE INTERNAT   AUSTIN   TX

From	Carrier	Class	Transaction Amount
DALLAS/FT WORTH TX			
To J F KENNEDY A/P NY	AA	MB	350.00
To PHILADELPHIA PA	22	V3	
To DALLAS/FT WORTH TX	AA	MB	Amount Use Only
To			9263001105664
			002700
			CO 265003

PASSENGER TICKET
S/E # 7992700005

ITEM 13 $350.00
AMERICAN AIRLINES   AUSTIN   TX

Cardmember Account No.	Transaction Date	Ticket Number
3783-647338-93038	09/17/93	0011350611A492

Passenger Name   Ticketing Airline
AHMAD/O   AMERICAN AIRLINES

Travel Agency Name   Issue Address
TRAVELSCOPE INTERNAT   AUSTIN   TX

From	Carrier	Class	Transaction Amount
DALLAS/FT WORTH TX			
To PHILADELPHIA PA	AA	MB	350.00
To DALLAS/FT WORTH TX	AA	MB	
To			Amount Use Only
To			9263001105668
			002700
			CO 265003

PASSENGER TICKET
S/E # 7992700006

ITEM 14 $392.00
UNITED AIRLINES   AUSTIN   TX

Cardmember Account No.	Transaction Date	Ticket Number
3783-647338-93038	09/17/93	0161350611A511

Passenger Name   Ticketing Airline
AHMAD/O   UNITED AIRLINES

Travel Agency Name   Issue Address
TRAVELSCOPE INTERNAT   AUSTIN   TX

From	Carrier	Class	Transaction Amount
SAN FRANCISCO CA			
To DULLES ARPT DC	UA	VE	392.00
To PHILADELPHIA PA	UA	VE	
To O HARE FIELD IL	UA	VE	9263906786087
To SAN FRANCISCO CA	UA	VE	003700
			CO 265003

PASSENGER TICKET
S/E # 7992700086

ITEM 15 $392.00
UNITED AIRLINES   AUSTIN   TX

Cardmember Account No.	Transaction Date	Ticket Number
3783-647338-93038	09/17/93	0161350611A522

Passenger Name   Ticketing Airline
BARAKJ/A   UNITED AIRLINES

Travel Agency Name   Issue Address
TRAVELSCOPE INTERNAT   AUSTIN   TX

From	Carrier	Class	Transaction Amount
SAN FRANCISCO CA			
To DULLES ARPT DC	UA	VE	392.00
To PHILADELPHIA PA	JA	VE	
To O HARE FIELD TL	UA	VE	9263906786088
To SAN FRANCISCO CA	UA	VE	003700
			CO 265003

PASSENGER TICKET
S/E # 7992700099

ITEM 16 $51.79
BIZMART   01313 RICHARDSON   TX

Cardmember Account No.	Date of Charge	Reference Code	Approval Code
3783-647338-93038	09/22/93	0059717715	

Service Establishment and Location
BIZMART   01313 RICHARDSON   TX

Record of Charge

OFFICE EQUIP/SUPPLIES

S/E #   1425598576

TOTAL CHARGE AMOUNT   **$51.79**

ITEM 17 $116.41
COURTYARD IDN   PHILADELPH   PA

Cardmember Account No.	Date of Charge	Reference Code	Approval Code
3783-647338-93038	10/03/93	003100007	

Service Establishment and Location
COURTYARD IDN   PHILADELPH   PA

Record of Charge

ARRIVAL DATE   DEPARTURE DATE
10/01/93   10/03/93

NSL   0001032

12

S/E #   2370304776

TOTAL CHARGE AMOUNT   **$116.41**

Q. If I can interrupt you for a moment. Where have we seen Omar Ahmad's name on the Elbarasse documents?

A. Well, he was listed with the IAP, but also with the Palestine Committee, on the Elbarasse list of Palestinian Committee members and the Ashqar list of Palestinian Committee members.

Q. And was he involved in that planning phone call that we played for this meeting?

A. Yes, he was.

Q. You testified that these are the HLF AMEX records?

A. Yes.

Q. Was Omar Ahmad an employee of the HLF?

A. No, he was not.

Q. Was he a board member?

A. No.

Q. Was he an officer?

A. No.

Q. Based upon the material that you reviewed, did he have any role with the HLF?

A. Only in respect to his role in the Palestinian Committee.

Q. Okay. Thank you.

MR. JONAS: If we can turn to page 14, please.

...

Q. Outside of the meeting did any of the Defendants publicly discuss what the purpose of the meeting was?

A. Yes.

Q. Who?

A. Shukri Abu Baker.

Q. If you have before you Baker Declaration, which is already in evidence.

A. I do. Bear with me one second while I find it.

Q. Sure.

A. I have it.

18

MR. JONAS: If we can turn to the third page, please, and put that on the screen.

Q. (BY MR. JONAS) The bottom half where it says F, can you read that, please, Agent Burns?

A. Yes. He says in his sworn statement, "The 1993 Philadelphia meeting was a meeting of Islamic intellectuals, academicians, community leaders, and representatives of American Islamic organizations, such as ours. It was not a meeting of any organization. No decisions were made by any organization about anything. Everyone there spoke their minds."

Q. At the Philly meeting was there an announcement made as to the actual purpose of the meeting?

A. Yes.

MR. JONAS: Your Honor, if we can play Philly Meeting 1 the first tape, segment B, please. (Whereupon, Philly Meeting No. 1, Segment B was played, while questions were propounded.)

Om: May God reward you well. Brother Abou Ibrahim should have been with us, but may God heal him. He is at the hospital for those who don't know. He had a surgery yesterday. So, we ask God the Almighty to heal him. This meeting was called for by the Palestine Committee in order to have a seminar or a meeting to the brothers present here today in order to study the situation in light of the latest developments on the Palestinian arena, its effects and impact on our work here in America. We wanted this program to be a quick one so that we could implement what we get out from this meeting in our upcoming festivals and in our activities which will begin, or which have begun last week and which will continue until the end of the year. Also, we wanted to present some strategies for work in the future. So, we found some points which we asked all the brothers to look at some or all of them. They are: Political activism and public relations, popular activism, charity work, media work. ...UI some papers which I have and brought them. I think that our work at the Association [Islamic Association for Palestine] or what we did at the Association is a responsibility which falls on all of our shoulders and we wanted to distribute this responsibility on all the brothers who are here today to bear the burden of what is going on.

. . . . Basically, the seminar is divided into four sessions; 3 sessions today and 1 session tomorrow, Sunday. Suggested time of the sessions are as follows: from 10-1, from 2-5, from 7-11 and, tomorrow, from 8-12. The first session will discuss the general political atmosphere and its impact on work in America. We have some papers. Those who wrote some papers could present them up in this session and...UI, could be presented at this time. We need to assign a moderator for this session. The second session will be about charity work and its future in light of the changes, it will be in the afternoon. There are papers to be presented and we will assign a moderator for this session. The third session is about political activism, media and popular activism and public relation in North America, the future and the challenges. It will be in the evening, God's willing, and we have papers to be presented...UI. Tomorrow, God's willing, the moderators of the three sessions today will be tomorrow's panel and will present .. I mean, the session's moderator is responsible for taking the session's minutes, determine the papers and come up with a final paper for the session. This paper will be presented to us and approved by us and, after he present this paper to us tomorrow, we will have 3 papers, not 1 page but 3 pages. Each one will present it and then we take action plan from it on what to do, visions and modify it then we approve it, that this what we came up with in that meeting.

Q. (BY MR. JONAS) Did you see where it says, "Abou Ibrahim should have been with us but he is at the hospital for those that don't know"?

A. Yes.

Q. Is that your explanation for why Mohamed El Mezain wasn't there, to your understanding?

A. Yes.

Q. In Shukri Baker's declaration did he say this is a meeting of the Palestine Committee?

A. No, he doesn't.

Q. I was corrected. This is the B clip, not the A clip. Does it say who the speaker is on the transcript? If it would help, I can give you mine.

A. I have it. Omar Ahmad.

Q. Okay. When Omar Ahmad announced that this was a meeting of the Palestine Committee, was Shukri Baker in the room?

A. Yes.

Q. How do you know that?

A. Because he spoke like within a minute before Omar Ahmad announced this.

MR. JONAS: If we can turn to page 3 of the excerpt. If we can get that on the screen, please, Philly meeting 1-E, page 3.

Q. (BY MR. JONAS) Do you see that, Agent Burns?

A. I do.

Q. Okay. Do we see Shukri Baker speaking?

A. Yes, we do.

Q. Does this area, this excerpt identify what his role is to be in this conference?

A. It does. It indicates that – would you like me to read it?

Q. Sure. Go ahead.

A. Omar Ahmad says, "The third session, who has papers? Gawad. The third session, who has papers for it? From the beginning, the first session we have Sheik Sharif and brother Abdel Salam, brother Gawad, and Aboul Hasan, Abdel Halim. Anyone else? Did you write them down? The second session, guys, stay with me so that we could finish. The second session we have Osama, Mo'een, and Shukri Abu Baker. And it will be about charity work. Anyone else? The third session will be about political media and popular activism and PR. We have Ghassan, Saleh, Gawad, and Abdel Rahman, Nihad and Akram. Anyone else? Who is going to be the moderator of the 1st session?" And he goes on, and down farther where Ghassan is speaking he says, "Regarding the 1st session, Shukri should be the moderator."

> The Nihad referenced here is Nihad Awad, co-founder and current Executive Director of CAIR. Nihad Awad was a member of the Islamic Association of Palestine, and is identified in the government's "Philly Meeting Summary" chart as "PC, CAIR" meaning Nihad Awad was known to the federal government as a member of the Palestine Committee. Awad's association with CAIR would lead to the decision by the FBI to end its ties to the CAIR National organization.[16]

Q. By the way, Agent Burns, does each transcript, for either the full transcript or the excerpted transcript, identify the speakers for that particular transcript?

A. Yes. On the very first page of each transcript.

Q. So where we have initials on the attributions as to who is speaking, all one has to do is go to the first page of the transcript and they can see who that person is. Is that correct?

A. That is correct. And with each transcript, different speakers will probably be identified. So on one transcript you may have five or six people, and on another transcript you may have ten people.

Q. And did Shukri Baker in fact moderate any sessions?

A. He did.

Q. Okay. Agent Burns, did Shukri Baker the Defendant talk about presenting a cover for this Philadelphia meeting in case anyone asks?

A. He did.

MR. JONAS: If we can turn to Philly Meeting No. 3.

Q. (BY MR. JONAS) Before I ask you about that one, did they jump around in subject matter during their sessions?

A. Yes. As you can see, the conference was organized into sessions according to topic, but they did venture off of topic on several occasions, and then they would try to get back on topic. But they do venture around.

Q. Okay. So we may venture around ourselves, then?

A. Yes, we will be doing that.

Q. Okay.

MR. JONAS: If we can turn to Philly Meeting No. 3, page 3. This is the excerpted one, Philly Meeting No. 3-E.

THE WITNESS: I have it.

Q. (BY MR. JONAS) Do can you have it before you?

A. I do.

Q. This is a short one so we will just read it. Do you see the second from the top segment? Can you read what Shukri Baker says about the meeting?

A. "My brothers, this talk is to be continued, God's willing. There are remarks now. Please don't mention the name Samah in an explicit manner. We agree on saying it as sister Samah. We will talk about her honor, and the session is – the session here is a joint workshop between the Holy Land Foundation and the IAP. This is the official form. I mean, please in case some inquired."

Q. Agent Burns, going back to your Philly Meeting Summary Chart, under organizations you list several organizations – PC, HLF, IAP, depending upon the individual. Can you explain that, please?

A. Yes. Individuals who are affiliated with various organizations, according to the evidence that has already been presented, their affiliations are noted in that column. For example, with the Defendant Shukri Abu Baker we have seen documents that we have are introduced here showing that he was

a member of the Palestinian Committee and the HLF, and we have seen his deposition testimony where he admitted being a member of the IAP's advisory board. Therefore, all three organizations are noted beside his name.

Q. Okay. And that continues throughout this chart?

A. That is correct.

Q. Okay. So Shukri Baker, what you just read, says, "In case someone inquired, the session here is a joint session between the Holy Land Foundation and the IAP." Is everyone who attended, pursuant to your summary, a member of the HLF or part of the HLF or the IAP?

A. No.

Q. Okay. He uses – He uses a term sister Samah. Does he talk about that in his declaration what sister Samah meant in this Philly conference?

A. In his sworn statement he does, yes.

MR. JONAS: If we can pull up Baker Declaration, page 4, please.

Q. (BY MR. JONAS) What does Shukri Baker say about the term Samah?

A. He says, "The use of the word Samah was a whimsical and ironic" –

MS. HOLLANDER: Would you have her read it from the beginning?

Q. (BY MR. JONAS) There is a word at the top right.

A. I am sorry. "Some people at the meeting spoke of Hamas openly, and there was no reason for them not to, since Hamas' role in Palestine was a natural subject of discussion, and Hamas was not a banned organization at that time. The use of the word Samah was a whimsical and ironic play on words. Samah means forgiveness in Arabic, and in my opinion those who used the term were making ironic fun of Hamas, not adopting a secret term to disguise their references to the organization."

Q. So, Agent Burns, in what we just read a moment ago when he says sister Samah, according to this declaration he is meaning sister forgiveness?

A. If you believe what he says in his declaration.

Q. Do you know what Samah is backwards?

A. Yes.

MR. JONAS: Your Honor, can I just use the elmo [sic], please?

23

Q. (BY MR. JONAS) Do you see what I wrote?

A. I do.

Q. What did I write? What word that is?

A. Reading left to right it is Samah.

Q. Okay. What is Samah backwards?

A. Hamas, which interestingly in reading Arabic you read from the right to the left.

MR. JONAS: Go back to the screen, please.

Q. (BY MR. JONAS) What meaning did the word Samah have in the conference?

A. It was a code word for Hamas.

Q. And is that identified in the conference?

A. Yes, it is.

MR. JONAS: Can you turn to Philly meeting 4-E? We are going to play segment A, please.

(Whereupon, Philly Meeting No. 4, Segment A was played, while questions were propounded.)

Q. (BY MR. JONAS) Agent Burns, have we seen any documents during the course of your testimony to indicate who was going to commit jihad to liberate Palestine?

A. Yes.

Q. What document?

A. Hamas, according to the Hamas charter.

Q. The first thing, or one of the first things we saw on that one, GA, which is who?

A. Gawad.

Q. Gawad says, "Hamas...the Samah Movement. I mean Samah." Did Shukri Baker express any concern over using the word Hamas during the course of this conference?

A. Yes, he did.

MR. JONAS: If we go back to Philly Meeting No. 3, page 3. This is a short one. The third segment.

Q. (BY MR. JONAS) Can you read that segment Agent Burns?

A. Yes. Let me find out who AU is. Aboul Osama is speaking. He says, "As far as the police is concerned, there is a good reaction to it. Expectations are that – It depends on the media if we managed to reach the people." An unknown male says, "What about people's opinions?" "That depends." Unknown male asks, "Is this against Hamas?" Shukri Abu Baker says, "Didn't we say not to mention that term?" Unknown male then says, "Is it against the Movement?"

Q. Agent Burns, have we seen the term Movement used in this case?

A. Yes, we have.

Q. What does that mean?

A. It is short for the Islamic Resistance Movement, which is Hamas.

Q. Is the Philadelphia meeting the only time you have seen the word Samah used?

A. No.

Q. When else have you seen it?

A. Phone calls.

Q. Do you have before you Baker Wiretap No. 4?

A. I do.

Q. And who are the participants on that call?

A. Shukri Abu Baker the Defendant, and Abdel Haleem Ashqar.

Q. What is the date of the call?

A. January 11th, 1996.

MR. JONAS: Your Honor, at this time I would offer into evidence Baker Wiretap No. 4 and 4-A.

THE COURT: Admitted.

MR. JONAS: If we can play that, please.

(Whereupon, Baker Wiretap No. 4, 4-A was played, while questions were propounded.)

Q. (BY MR. JONAS) Agent Burns, do you see where Shukri Baker says, "visited their aunt's house"?

A. I do.

Q. Have you seen that term used before?

A. I have.

Q. Where?

A. I have seen it in some of the evidence here; none that we have discussed yet.

Q. Without giving your understanding of it, is it a word that – In the context that you have seen it, not just in this call, but other contexts, is that a code word?

26

A. It is a code word.

Q. Okay. Agent Burns, do you see where it says, "he claims a relation to her, this Hajja Samah"?

A. I do.

Q. Using the definition as applied in Baker's declaration, the sworn statement, would that mean Hajja forgiveness?

A. If you look at his statement, but it makes no sense in this context.

Q. Have you seen the term Hajja before?

A. Yes.

Q. Do you know what that means?

A. It can be translated as sister. It is more of a respected female, but it can be translated as sister.

MS. CADEDDU: I object to her opining about what things mean in Arabic. She is not an expert or translator. She doesn't speak Arabic.

THE COURT: Overrule that objection. She may testify to her understanding. Go ahead.

Q. (BY MR. JONAS) And is sister Samah the term that we have seen used in the Philadelphia meeting?

A. It is.

Q. Agent Burns, do you see the term "old man"?

A. I do.

Q. Have you seen that term used before?

A. I have seen that term used in the context of this issue and this evidence to mean Yasser Arafat.

Q. Agent Burns, have you seen the use of the term Samah in other calls?

A. Yes.

Q. We will save them for later.

A. Okay.

Q. All right. You testified that at the time of the Philadelphia meeting the Oslo Accords had just come out. Correct?

A. That is correct.

Q. Per the Hamas charter, what was Hamas' position on the Oslo Accords?

A. Well, according to the Hamas charter they were opposed to any type of peaceful compromise with the Israelis. The charter predated the Oslo Accords, the signing of the Oslo Accords.

Q. Did the participants in the Philadelphia meeting discuss moving in the same direction as Hamas on this issue?

A. They did.

MR. JONAS: If we can play Philly Meeting No. 2-E, Segment A, please. (Whereupon, Philly Meeting No. 2-E, Segment A was played, while questions were propounded.)

We must not deal with it unless to the extent which facilitates activism and does not affect the fundamentals. This is everything in that regards. The relationship between the

different active organizations must be re-examined in light of the new directions in order to be truly organized, effective, wholesome, complete and in a legal form as they...UI. They must remain separate and don't bear responsibility for each other. In addition to the direction in place, the following should be noted: determining organizations which can contribute to dealing with the new reality based on the previous approaches such as the Fund, the [Islamic] Association [for Palestine] or a large organization in one of the forms which were mentioned, determining the role assigned to each organization and its relationships with the other organizations, both formal and informal relationships, the available capabilities for activism ...UI for each organization. What are its capabilities and can it continue working in the long or the short term, to what extent. The challenges which face each organization and how to counter them from the practical aspect. An internal challenge, a challenge with the community, a challenge with the Movement, a challenge with the...UI, a challenge with the media. The programs of the organizations overall should be in complete harmony with the general directions of the Movement. I say that once again because this is very important. By "harmony" I mean that they ought to serve it in a direct or an indirect manner. But, the format is the flexible part. The...UI in the West should be taken into consideration and the available capabilities. But, what is important is that all the programs and the lines are serving the general direction on the short and the long term. This requires reviewing the general directions...UI. God's willing, they will be available for review. It must be noted that it is important that the organizations provide opinion and information the Islamic Movement. I tell you simply,

Q. (BY MR. JONAS) Agent Burns, what is the Fund?

A. That is the Holy Land Foundation.

Q. Agent Burns, do you see where it says, "The programs or the organizations overall should be in complete harmony with the general directions of the Movement"? What is the Movement?

A. The Islamic Resistance Movement, Hamas.

Q. Who is Abou Ibrahim?

A. The Defendant Mohamed El Mezain.

Q. Agent Burns, the individual I believe was Gawad who was speaking, talked about moving in directions. They talked about the Movement being Hamas. Did Defendant Shukri Baker also talk about moving in particular directions?

A. He did.

MR. JONAS: Okay. If you will turn to Philly Meeting No. 6-E. If we can play Segment A, please.

(Whereupon, Philly Meeting No. 6-E, Segment A was played, while questions were propounded.)

Audio file: MTGB_19931002_4.WAV

Sh: ... So, the ramifications of the current political situation on activism on America..., I imagine, my brothers, that if we examine our work in America to the light..., that is; sum it as organizational activism, we exist in the shape of organizations in America. IAP works as an organization and we have the Fund. You could probably put the IAP and the Fund together and everything else that is in the paper, i.e. ...UI, the relationship with the Fund...UI. So, if you have noticed, in the past time, we used to focus on..., or the address was directed to the Palestinian and Islamic public, truly, in particular. We used to have an approach which probably had a glaring color, I mean the Jihadist [*address*] and this and that, focus on activism even through our lectures, conferences and seminars. And maybe this address was in harmony with the current, the general current was marching in that direction. Therefore, we were marching in that direction. We used to tell the Islamic and the Palestinian communities about the heroism of the youths in the inside. They used to be happy and we encouraged them...

Om: [*i.e.*] Military upbringing.

Sh: What?

Om: Military breeding.

Q. (BY MR. JONAS) Who is speaking here?

A. This is the Defendant Shukri Abu Baker.

Q. Okay. Agent Burns, do you see where Shukri Baker says, "We used to have an approach which probably had a glaring color, I mean, the jihadist [address], and this and that, focus on activism even through our lectures, conferences and seminars"? You said you viewed videotapes, which we have seen some, and I assume we will see more.

A. Yes.

Q. In those videotapes, did many of them predate the Philadelphia conference?A. They do.

Q. The ones that predate Philadelphia, are they of the same nature of the ones we saw already talking about Hamas, Hamas symbols on the screen, et cetera?

A. The ones that predate the Philadelphia meeting, yes.

Q. The ones that postdate Philadelphia, does the nature of them change?

A. Yes. They are very toned down.

Q. Did you hear the Defendant Shukri Baker use the term "derailment"?

A. Yes.

Q. Used it a few times. Is that correct?

A. That is correct.

Q. Did any of the other participants discuss derailment?

A. Yes.

...

Q. (BY MR. JONAS) Agent Burns, before the break we had played a statement where the Defendant Shukri Baker used the term derailment a few times. And I believe I asked you, was the term derailment used which other participants in this Philadelphia meeting?

A. Yes, it was.

Q. What was the context?

A. They were discussing how to derail the Oslo Peace Accords.

...

Q. (BY MR. JONAS) During back to the Philadelphia meeting, did the Defendant Shukri Abu Baker discuss the support that the organizations must give to Hamas?

A. Yes.

MR. JONAS: If we can go to Philly Meeting No. 12, Segment A, please, from the excerpt.

(Whereupon, Philly Meeting No. 12, Segment A was played, while questions were propounded.)

Sh: As a direction. We're not..., we're not putting the plan in place. As a direction. Is it Ok that from now on we start thinking that the children of the community should be steered towards media, journalism and law and then tell them to go live in the homeland. Very general talk which we didn't say four years ago. We say it now. As for how the plan is going to be and these details will come later. This is just the general direction. Is it acceptable?

Group: Yes.

Sh: More than one brother focused on it yesterday and we saw that it is good to... That's it. Ok, our brothers, there are things to say in regards to our strategy relating to the peace project that it must be focused on the most the project can achieve. For instance, the brother said that the most it can achieve is the Palestinian state. Based on that, we examine the facts relating to the Palestinian state so that when the Palestinian state takes form, huh, we are already ahead of it and we are not still talking about self-rule. The self-rule is finished. What's after that? So, this was... But, do you think this is going to be discussed?

Gh: No.

UM: This is a sub-item under the media aspect.

Sh: Let's leave it to the brothers who are called the Think Tank, our politicians who keep working on this issue.

UM: The Association.

Om: ...UI.

Sh: The idea that media should adopt that, the idea to highlight the notion that Islamists.... the Islamists - we know what we mean by the Islamists - are the alternative, the alternative with a definite article. This is my opinion and I think we should take a vote on it because there are our brothers who can write about these issues.

Q. (BY MR. JONAS) Again, Agent Burns, what is the Movement?

A. That is the Islamic Resistance Movement, Hamas.

Q. Agent Burns, how does Shukri Baker refer to what is going on with the Oslo Accords in this attribution right here?

A. In this attribution he refers to the Oslo Accords as the peace project.

Q. Agent Burns, based upon your review of the Elbarasse records, which are in evidence here, was there one of the organizations of the Palestine Committee that functioned as a think tank?

A. The United Association for Studies and Research was what its title said, a research center, which would be a think tank.

> *The United Association for Studies and Research was established by Hamas leader Mousa Abu Marzook, and employed a number of individuals who would later go on to play key roles at CAIR including Nabil Sadoun, and CAIR research director Mohammed Nimer.[17]*

...

Q. Did any of the participants in the Philadelphia meeting discuss how they would go about supporting the resistance?

A. They did.

MR. JONAS: If we can play Segment G of Philly Meeting No. 5.

(Whereupon, Philly Meeting No. 5, Segment G was played, while questions were propounded.)

Ga: Even supporting Hamas. The [*Islamic*] Association [*for Palestine*] met with the FBI in defense of Hamas. It was a clear talk then. Support to the Movement. Henceforth, do these goals mean anything?

UM2: Keep your voice down. May God be pleased with you.

[*Laughter*].

Sh: You Virginia guys got us trouble. This is the talk we will...

Sh: Before..., before all of that talk we should ask ourselves a question; Is America a confrontation front? And what do we want from..., from the reader of Al Zaytouna and the reader of the Monitor and from the guy who owns a store in Chicago? Do I want him to go fight or do I want to earn his sympathy so that he could donate to me or do I want him to have a knowledgeable political culture? We have to specify what we want from people, honestly, otherwise we keep working and publishing a newspaper becomes a goal in itself without finding out what effect does the newspaper have on people. I believe before this session is over we should come up with a clear statement regarding what do we want from people. This is one. And what do we want from the Americans? Do we want to convert them to Muslims, to become Muslims, because the [*Islamic*] Association [*for Palestine*] often does activities which sound like that of mosques; pure Islamic things. ...' The second thing -we were talking about that in the morning- is that our brothers in the Occupied Territories will be pretend to go along with the self-rule and none of their societies will be shut down and this is a matter that hasn't been settled yet. Then enter our brothers who talk to us about politics and tell you: "It is impossible that there will be a self-rule. It is impossible that America will classify Samah as a terrorist organization. It is impossible that Israel will withdraw from one inch. Impossible, impossible....". My brothers, they say that there are no absolutes in politics to start with, there is nothing impossible in politics, everything is possible. It is possible that Israel withdraw tomorrow and forms a Palestinian state the way it wants. What is that? Is the Palestinian state going to be worse than Saudi Arabia. for instance? Saudi Arabia is serving Israel's interests more than Israel serving its own interests. What are you talking about? So, our brother is telling you "Instead of being taken by surprise and then, five months later, begin to wail..", he said: "We will form an organization for you to show the Americans that you are...UI. It will be made up of some of our people, our beloved ones, and let's not hoist a large Islamic flag and let's not be barbaric-talking. We will remain a front so that if the thing happens, we will benefit from the new happenings instead of

---

Q. (BY MR. JONAS) Agent Burns, where the Defendant Shukri Abu Baker says, "You Virginia guys got us in trouble," were there people from Virginia who attended this meeting?

A. Yes.

Q. Who?

A. One of them was Muin Shabib was in Virginia at that time.

Q. How about Elbarasse?

A. He was as well.

Q. Did any of the participants, in particular the Defendant Shukri Abu Baker, express any concern about Hamas being labeled as a terrorist organization?

A. They did.

MR. JONAS: If we can play Philly No. 5, Segment H. (Whereupon, Philly Meeting No. 5, Segment H was played, while questions were propounded.)

Sh: Before..., before all of that talk we should ask ourselves a question; Is America a confrontation front? And what do we want from..., from the reader of Al Zaytouna and the reader of the Monitor and from the guy who owns a store in Chicago? Do I want him to go fight or do I want to earn his sympathy so that he could donate to me or do I want him to have a knowledgeable political culture? We have to specify what we want from people, honestly, otherwise we keep working and publishing a newspaper becomes a goal in itself without finding out what effect does the newspaper have on people. I believe before this session is over we should come up with a clear statement regarding what do we want from people. This is one. And what do we want from the Americans? Do we want to convert them to Muslims, to become Muslims, because the [Islamic] Association [for Palestine] often does activities which sound like that of mosques; pure Islamic things. ...'   The second thing -we were talking about that in the morning- is that our brothers in the Occupied Territories will be pretend to go along with the self-rule and none of their societies will be shut down and this is a matter that hasn't been settled yet. Then enter our brothers who talk to us about politics and tell you: "It is impossible that there will be a self-rule. It is impossible that America will classify Samah as a terrorist organization. It is impossible that Israel will withdraw from one inch. Impossible, impossible....". My brothers, they say that there are no absolutes in politics to start with, there is nothing impossible in politics, everything is possible. It is possible that Israel withdraw tomorrow and forms a Palestinian state the way it wants. What is that? Is the Palestinian state going to be worse than Saudi Arabia, for instance? Saudi Arabia is serving Israel's interests more than Israel serving its own interests. What are you talking about? So, our brother is telling you "Instead of being taken by surprise and then, five months later, begin to wail..", he said: "We will form an organization for you to show the Americans that you are...UI. It will be made up of some of our people, our beloved ones, and let's not hoist a large Islamic flag and let's not be barbaric-talking. We will remain a front so that if the thing happens, we will benefit from the new happenings instead of

This statement by Shukri Abu Baker is very interesting, and reflects the shift taking place in the nature of Muslim Brotherhood activity in the United States in this period. Regarding the U.S. being a "Confrontation front" we know from other Muslim Brotherhood documents that the Brotherhood engaged in paramilitary style training at campgrounds in the United States at least as late as 1982. [18] *This was not their primary activity however, and training was likely aimed at preparing Brothers for jihadist activities abroad, and not U.S.-based activity.* [19] *Instead the primary goals of the Brotherhood during this period focused on establishing networks of organizations and political fronts. In 1991, U.S. Muslim Brotherhood leader Mohammed Akram Adlouni authored "An*

Explanatory Memorandum on the General Strategic Goal for the Brotherhood in North America". The Explanatory Memorandum reflected the goals of a 1987 long-term Brotherhood to insure the Muslim Brotherhood dominated the American Muslim community through the control of Islamic Centers, schools and mosques, with an end goal of undermining and "sabotaging" U.S. society through what it described as a "civilizational jihadist process."[20] In 1993, AbuBaker seems to be considering how best to reconcile overarching U.S. Muslim Brotherhood policy goals with the Palestine Committee's primary responsibility of supporting Hamas; hence the references to the Islamic Association for Palestine's performance of "activities like that of mosques..."

Q. (BY MR. JONAS) Agent Burns, did you see where it says Al Zatounia?

A. I do.

Q. Have we seen Al Zatounia referenced in the Elbarasse records?

A. I believe it was referenced in one of the documents as one of the periodicals.

Q. Periodicals published by whom?

A. The IAP.

MR. JONAS: Play the next segment, Philly No. 5, Segment I. (Whereupon, Philly Meeting No. 5, Segment I was played, while questions were propounded.)

Q. (BY MR. JONAS) Agent Burns, you see where Shukri Baker – Is he the one speaking?

A. He is.

Q. He talks about "Our brothers in the occupied territories will pretend to go along with the self-rule, and none of their societies will be shut down." During the course of your testimony have we talked about any societies that belong to Hamas?

A. The Islamic Center of Gaza would be one.

Q. That was the one that was founded by Sheikh Yassin?

A. That is correct. That the HLF gave money to in the early years.

Q. Agent Burns, do you see where Shukri Baker uses the word Samah again?

A. I do.

Q. And under his definition would that say, then, "America will classify forgiveness as a terrorist organization," if you used the definition he provided in his declaration?

A. If you use the definition he provided in his sworn declaration, in this context it makes no sense.

Q. Agent Burns, are you familiar with the al-Aqsa educational that is in quotes there?

A. I am.

Q. Is that an entity we are going to talk about in a little while?

A. That is an entity that we actually spoke about on Thursday, Abdel Haleem Ashqar's educational fund.

Q. Ashqar is again who?

A. A member of the Palestine Committee.

Q. He was a participant in the Philadelphia meeting?

A. That is correct.

MR. JONAS: If we can play from Philly Meeting No. 5, Section J. (Where upon, Philly Meeting No. 5, Section J was played, while questions were propounded.)

Sh: Samah..., Samah is classified as a terrorist [*organization*]. By constitution, by law, if I wanted to adopt its work, they kick me out, they kick me out of this country, my brother. By God, they would take away my U.S. citizenship and tell me "Go away". I'm telling you....

Ga: We are not classified, my brother. Who said we are classified?

Sh: Huh?

Ga: Who classified it?

Sh: ...er. I'm saying..., I'm saying that even...

Ga: ...UI that the Movement is a terrorist organization.

Om: No, no, no.

Sh: ...UI, my brother. What did the Congress do?

Ga: There isn't a proposition to... What did it do?

Om: ...UI. The bill didn't pass.

Ga: Huh?

Om: It didn't come yet. The Congress bill didn't...

Ga: It is proposed.

Sh: You mean they won't classify it?

Om: God knows. Basically, let's stay with the..., let's stay on the media topic.

Sh: I was bringing it up in a sarcastic way because every time our problem is that we are reactive, reactive, reactive. Let's be - just one time in our lives - expect the worst case scenario and be proactive so that when an event takes place we would have a blanket to fall on instead of falling to the ground. That's all I mean. That's it.

Q. (BY MR. JONAS) Agent Burns, at the time of the Philadelphia meeting in 1993, had Hamas been officially designated as a terrorist organization by the United States?

A. No. Actually the mechanism for designating an organization as a terrorist did not exist at the time of this conference.

Q. Are you aware if the United States in any way recognized Hamas as a terrorist organization at around this time?

A. After the Oslo Accords, the U.S. State Department came out and named them as a terrorist organization, but it did not have the same effect as what an official designation would later on.

Q. What was that document that it came out in?

A. Generally they print these things in what is called –They have a pamphlet called The Patterns of Global Terrorism.

MR. JONAS: Finally, if we can turn to Philly Meeting No. 6 and play segment D.

(Whereupon, Philly Meeting NO. 6, Segment D was played, while questions were propounded.)

Sh: The other issue..., not necessarily now, the other issue my brother is the legal and security situation. I mean, now you don't resist only..., only..., you resist the entire world, the whole world now. The entire world is against you, the whole world is against you. No doubt, there will be legal obstacles. Three years ago, we were visited by some of our brothers ...UI and we said "Our brothers, think about the day Sister Samah will get divorced, when everybody rejects her and say about her that she is a terrorist". They were saying that this will never happen. This a country of laws and a country of constitution and it did happen. So, you work and you try to protect. You are trying to get her married again. Are you really going to remain respected in the eyes of the law or there will be another talk? I hope that the brothers..., we can talk about that for half an hour. I hope the brothers think about this issue...UI. Go ahead, Abou Mohamad. There will also be a discussion...UI.

Q. (BY MR. JONAS) Agent Burns, who is speaking now?

A. This is the Defendant Shukri Abu Baker.

Q. Okay. Agent Burns, did the participants discuss what they can and cannot say to America?

A. They did.

MR. JONAS: If we can play Philly Meeting No. 6, segment E. (Whereupon, Philly Meeting No. 6, Segment E was played, while questions were propounded.)

Q. (BY MR. JONAS) Agent Burns, who is speaking now?

A. This speaker is an unidentified male.

Q. Agent Burns, are you familiar with what is termed the 1948 territories?

A. Yes.

Q. What does that mean? What is your understanding of what that means?

A. That means Israel as it exists. Israel was established in 1948, so if you are requesting the 1948 territories you want the land that is now considered Israel.

Q. Agent Burns, what document have we seen that discusses demanding the 1948 territories?

A. The Hamas charter.

Q. Are there other times when they discuss what they can and cannot say to the Americans?

A. Yes.

MR. JONAS: If we can play Philly Meeting No. 7, Segment A. (Whereupon, Philly Meeting No. 7, Segment A was played, while questions were propounded.)

UM2:   ...: I mean if we fail in this country it means that our entire cause will fail. I started to get this feeling, really. This new organization..., brother Shukri is discussing it in a way while brother Ghassan looks at it in a different way. But, there is one conclusion we will get out of this organization which is confusing the Islamic mentality here in America. The Islamic mentality in America will be confused. It is already confused. A lot of you will say "Confused? How come? They are already confused". But, you have to understand that in case it wanted to win the general public opinion here in America..., in case the other organization was hit or stuff, it can issue a statement saying "By God, we are in agreement. We are in agreement on this and in agreement on that". And those who read your stuff..., who reads your stuff? This is a question we must ask ourselves. Who is going to read your ads and your statements? The only thing people will see is that there is a new organization - and it is not known what it is - which writes articles about the issue of the new Palestinian state. And you could try to convince people from behind [*saying*] "Tone it down a little". Thus, you want to address the enemy while you are speaking to your friend and this friend of yours doesn't...UI. Our brothers, my opinion is - and God knows best - that we don't discuss the goals but focus very much on what we have in the discussion, arrange our priorities in a good way and go on with that and there is no need for new organizations or stuff. Let's be distinguished, God's willing, in a way which will get us out of this crisis, God's willing.

Sh: ...UI. [*Laughter*].

UM1: God's willing we will...UI. I would like to ask brother Omar about two points in that regards.

Om: Go ahead.

UM1: The first point is: Have you studied the legal status of the [*Islamic*] Association [*for Palestine*] in light of its address and found there are real dangers such as closing the [*Islamic*] Association [*for Palestine*] soon, for instance, any time soon?

Om: By God, I will tell you where the danger is. The danger is two-fold, either a financial connection or orders.

UM1: Hum.

Q. (BY MR. JONAS) Who is speaking here?

A. This is an unknown male.

Q. And this unknown male refers to Shukri. Was there any other Shukri at the Philadelphia meeting besides the Defendant Shukri Baker?

A. No.

Q. Agent Burns, you see where it says, "You can try to convince people from behind saying tone it down a little"?

A. I do.

Q. Is that consistent with what you testified earlier about the videotapes of the conferences, toning it down post Philadelphia meeting?

40

A. Yes.

Q. Agent Burns, do you see – Who is OM that is speaking?

> Om: I mean if you work for someone overseas and he gives you orders to carry out. These are the only two dangers.
>
> UM1: Yes.
>
> Om: The issue is that if you cover these two bases, you will find that you, as an American organization, can do whatever you want. This is from legal point of view. As for the media, it is possible that you could be destroyed by the media without the law touching you.
>
> Sh: Aha.
>
> Om: For instance, newspapers and magazines can say that you are a terrorist because you are an Islamic organization...
>
> UM1: Yes, I understand.
>
> Om: I mean, they could hold things against you and destroy you on the media front before you're destroyed by the government and the law. This is like Sheik Omar, for instance.
>
> UM1: Yes.
>
> Om: Sheik Omar Abdel Rahman, there are no..., what you call crimes against him, you see?
>
> UM1: Yes.
>
> Om: Other than they kept digging around him and stuff like that. But, it was the media which accused him before he was legally charged and he wasn't able to..., because he didn't have a support system. He couldn't defend himself in face of the media. The media is overwhelming, that is. So, what I can say is that our problem at the [Islamic] Association [for Palestine] is the following: the problem is the address; if you want to the Americans, you lose the Muslims. If you address the Muslims, it means that you cannot reveal your address to the Americans. Frankly speaking.
>
> UM1: Yes.

A. That is Omar Ahmad.

Q. Do you see where he references Sheik Omar Abdel Rahman?

A. I do.

Q. Do you know who that individual is?

A. Yes.

Q. Who is that?

A. He is one of the individuals who is currently incarcerated for his role in the plotting of the first World Trade Center bombing.

Q. Which occurred in the early '90s?

A. In 1993.

Q. He is not a member of the Palestine Committee, is he?

A. No, he is not.

Q. Was he part of this meeting at all?

A. No, he was not.

Q. Other than a reference to him here, does he have any involvement to the Defendants, based upon the evidence that you have seen?

A. Not based on the evidence that we have discussed, no.

> Sheikh Omar Abdel Rahman, known as the Blind Sheikh, was convicted of seditious conspiracy for his role in the 1993 World Trade Center bombing as well as for his role in the foiled "New York City Landmarks plot." Abdel Rahman was found guilty of "conspir[ing] to overthrow, or put down, or destroy by force the Government of the United States."[21] While Burns notes that Abdelrahman shared no direct involvement with the Holy Land Foundation or its founders, the two cases did share unindicted co-conspirators, including Philly Meeting attendees Mohammed Al-Hanooti, and the co-founder of both Hamas and Al Qaeda, Abdullah Azzam. 1993 WTC bombing unindicted co-conspirator Sirraj Wahhaj would also serve as a member of the board of advisors while Omar Ahmad served as CAIR National Chairman.[22]

Q. (BY MR. JONAS) Did the Defendant Shukri Abu Baker discuss deception?

A. He did.

Q. If we can, staying with Philly Meeting No. 7, do you have page 6 before you?

A. I do.

Q. We will put it on the screen and read this one. It is fairly short. I believe it is page 5, the second segment there. Who is speaking?

A. That is the Defendant Shukri Abu Baker.

Q. Okay. Can you read this segment?

A. He says, "I swear by your God that war is deception. War is deception. We are fighting our enemy with a kind heart and we never thought of deceiving it. War is deception. Deceive, camouflage, pretend that you're leaving while you're walking that way. Or do we have to be – Deceive your enemy." Omar Ahmad says, "This is like one who plays basketball. He makes a player believe that he is doing this while he does something else. I agree with you. Like they say, politics is a completion of war." Shukri Abu Baker says, "Yes, politics, like war, is a deception."

> *Shukri Abu Baker was like paraphrasing a hadith, a reported saying of the prophet of Islam Mohammed used as part of the source texts for Sharia, Islamic law. Mohammed reportedly said, "War is Deceit", as recorded in the Bukhari hadith collection.*[23]

Q. Agent Burns, in 1993 when the Philadelphia meeting took place, what was the Holy Land Foundation supposed to be?

A. A Muslim charity.

Q. Did this discussion of war being deception come up again?

A. It did.

MR. JONAS: If we can turn to Philly Meeting No. 12-E. If we can play Segment E of Philly meeting 12.

(Whereupon, Philly Meeting No. 12-E, Segment E was played, while questions were propounded.)

UM: In the name of God, the Beneficent, the Merciful. God's willing, I will begin with a summary of the 3rd session yesterday which was about political, media and public action in America which is the future and the challenges. In reality, I summarized it in three or four elements, a simple introduction and goals of the coming stage, priorities of action, axises of action and specific recommendations based on the stuff that was mentioned yesterday. In the name of God, the Beneficent, the Merciful. It is expected that the last goals are a reflection for political, media and public action in America due to the U.S. Administration's complete support to the agreement and the Jewish influence on the media outlets with that is based on that such as the impact on the Islamic, Palestinian and Arab community. Therefore, goals of the Palestinian action must be explained in the coming stage on the U.S. front and determine possible means to achieve these goals. I wrote six goals and we can discuss them one by one based on what was presented yesterday. The first goal is to continue to support the Palestinian cause and defending the Movement's positions and explaining them in the suitable way at the Palestinian, Arab and Islamic community's level and the American people in order to form a public opinion which adopts the Movement's position and its political program using the available resources. Of course, through the address. By the way, we will be discussing the issue of the political address later. Would you like to present this point for discussion or continue?

Gh: It is agreed upon.

UM: Agreed upon. Ok. Two, working to stabilize Islamic organizations working for Palestine and protecting them under a legal cover to guarantee their continuity in conducting their mission. Agreed upon or...?

Om: Keep going.

UM: Yes. Three, strengthening..., strengthening our presence in the Palestinian, Arab and Islamic community and resorting to all possible means to maintain the current gains, developing them and strengthening the alliance with Arab and Islamic organizations in the field. Ok? Four, working to make the Islamic Association for Palestine the main source of information which represents the Movement's positions.

Q. (BY MR. JONAS) Agent Burns, who is speaking here?

A. I believe it was – I need to look at the beginning of it, or if you can tell me what page it is on in the transcript.

Q. On the excerpt it is page 6.

A. Unknown male.

Q. Okay. You see he says, "The first goal is to continue to support the Palestinian cause and defending the Movement's positions," what is the Movement?

A. The Islamic Resistance Movement, Hamas.

Q. Agent Burns, do you see where it says, "Working to make the Islamic Association for Palestine the main source of information which represents the movement's positions," who published the Hamas charter in the United States?

44

UM: Of course, regarding the point which was mentioned yesterday that when we fight with the other Islamic organizations, it weakens our position and our political address. ...about the Movement's position of the cause and this in order to make sure to continue to offer a clear Islamic position to the Islamic community. A special focus on the Islamic community while being careful not to show the Association as an opposition party with direct connections with the inside. It expresses its position. It expresses the Movement's position but it doesn't say I represent this side or anything like that.

Sh: It should lie, you mean.

UM: It shouldn't talk [*laughter*]. It shouldn't lie. It shouldn't talk [*laughter*].

Sh: War is deception.

Om: Learn from your masters in the Fund [*laughter*].

A. The IAP.

Q. Is that the Islamic Association for Palestine?

A. Yes, it is.

Q. Agent Burns, who is SH that says "It should lie"?

A. That is the Defendant Shukri Abu Baker.

Q. Agent Burns, did you see where it said, "Learn from your masters in the Fund"? What is the Fund?

A. The Holy Land Foundation.

Q. Agent Burns, do you have the last page of Philly segment 12-E before you? There is just one line there that is the last segment?

A. I do.

MR. JONAS: If we can put that last page, page 8 open the screen, please.

Q. (BY MR. JONAS) Agent Burns, just one line. What does Shukri Baker say, the last line in the excerpted transcript?

A. He says, "Your mother Samah is the mother of democracy."

Q. Did Shukri Baker the Defendant say anything about what he can and cannot say to America about his relationship to Hamas?

A. He did.

MR. JONAS: If we turn to Philly Meeting No. 8, in the excerpts if you can turn to page 3. Can we get page 3 on the screen, please?

Q. (BY MR. JONAS) Agent Burns, starting with the top where it says UM, "I can repeat the text," can you read the rest of this segment please?

A. "I can repeat the text if that is going to solve the problem. We can say attacking the – the credibility of the representation of the Organization, the Organization's right to sign an accord on behalf of the Palestinian people."

Q. Let me pause you for a moment. Which organization signed the Oslo Accords on behalf of the Palestinian people?

A. The Palestine Liberation Organization.

Q. Okay. Continue.

A. Gawad says, "No, he didn't sign as the Organization. He signed as Abu Ammar. He didn't sign as the Organization." Unknown male says, "No, he signed the Palestinian people.

What's his name? Abu Abbas signed as the Palestinian delegation." Gawad said, "But not even one major democratic Palestinian organization until now has –" Unknown male says, "This is the point. This is the point." Shukri Abu Baker said, "This is what they understand – Abu, Abu. This is what they understand. Currently Abu Ammar is the chairman of the PLO. Our brothers, we cannot use the same poetic Arabic style when addressing the American mentality. Our brother, the American will not understand it. Please allow me. They will tell you, 'If he doesn't represent you, why the hell don't you get rid of him?' He will tell you, 'If he doesn't represent you, who represents the Palestinian people?'"

Unknown male says, "We should drop the Arafat issue now. We're talking about the Organization."

Shukri Abu Baker says, "These are very critical questions. We're replying to the question. It is very critical." Unknown male, "If he is democratic." Shukri Abu Baker says, "I cannot say to him that I'm Hamas."

MR. JONAS: If we play the next segment of Philly Meeting No. 8, which is Segment B. (Whereupon, Philly Meeting No. 8, Segment B was played, while questions were propounded.)

46

Q. (BY MR. JONAS) Agent Burns, do you see where it says, "I mean, in the same style as Samah's"?

A. Yes.

Q. Would that mean "in the same style of forgiveness"?

A. No, it doesn't.

Q. Who is speaking right now?

A. Shukri Abu Baker is.

Q. And Omar Yehia is who?

A. That is the same as Omar Ahmad the IAP member/Palestinian Committee member who has been speaking quite frequently throughout this.

Q. Shukri Baker says, "You can go meet a Congressman in your name, in Omar Yehia's name, in the name of the Association's present, and tell him [UI] doesn't represent us. Mr. Ahmad Yassin represents us." Who is Ahmed Yassin?

A. The Hamas founder, the former spiritual leader that is on your board there in the middle on the top.

Q. The top, Sheikh Ahmed Yassin?

A. That is correct.

> Operating under the CAIR brand, Omar Ahmad and his compatriots would indeed meet and seek to influence members of Congress. Individuals associated with CAIR have contributed a total of **$664,773** to congressional campaigns.[24] CAIR press releases routinely brag about the organization's ability to meet with and influence members of Congress.[25]While it's unclear what Omar Ahmad or other CAIR officials have said about their ties to Hamas' Sheikh Yassin -now deceased- in Congressional meetings, CAIR officials did affiliate on Capitol Hill with those who would later be identified as terrorists, such as CAIR executive director Nihad Awad and CAIR employee Ismail Royer attending a sermon by Al Qaeda ideologue Anwar Awlaki on Capitol Hill in 2001.[26]

MR. JONAS: If we can stay with Philly Meeting No. 8, page 5 of the Philly meeting 8-E, the excerpted portion, the top half, please.

Q. (BY MR. JONAS) Agent Burns, if you can read what Shukri Baker says at this point in the meeting?

A. He says, "The point you presented which is – which is withdrawing, attacking his credibility as a representative and a leader of the Palestinian people. But I tell you that we don't want the American front to become a front for direct conflict. These things will put us in direct conflict, not only with the Palestinians, even with the official government circles. What is our benefit? What is our interest? As Palestinian action organizations in America, what is our benefit in creating more enemies than necessary? What is the interest that – Are you going to win the Palestinian cause if this guy who works at McDonald's, the worker who works there for $4 an hour understands whether Abu Ammar represents us or not, or the Congressman? If you explain the situation to him that he is – and doesn't represent the Palestinian people, is he going to tell you, 'Yes, by God, you convinced me.' Despite that everything goes as planned. The point is that we are not going to expose ourselves to another wave and be anti-establishment – anti-establishment. Okay? Because for the American organizations, if you're against peace you're a terrorist. When you start attacking Abu Ammar, his leadership, the people who signed and attended and arranged their affairs with – such as a Saudi person who attacks the Saud family and say that he is not a ruler, my brother, let him –"Unknown male says, "Okay. Amazing. But brother, please finish."

Q. That is fine. Were there any other discussions regarding their presentation or their face to America?

A. Yes.

Q. Were there several more discussions regarding that topic?

A. Yes.

Q. In fact, was that the subject matter of this whole conference, this whole meeting?

A. Yes.

MR. JONAS: Let's look at one more. Philly Meeting No. 10 in the excerpt page 2. Can you get that on the screen, please, the bottom half?

Q. (BY MR. JONAS) Agent Burns, are you up to reading one more?

A. Okay. Gawad says, "America and the American, in order to convince the people, because everybody is convinced; the Americans are convinced and the Jews. People must – On the ground they're happy with the flag now, but the flag will last one week, two weeks, or a month. And what is after that? We need bread. This will be – The propaganda will be spread will affect Hamas. In the meanwhile, are you going to collect a million? Not a million for instance. The media and political support for the Cause in general terms, and to the rights of the Palestinian people specifically will be negatively affected in my opinion. Why? First, the organizations which work on these issues are American and they deal from the – from America's mentality. A prominent example for that is the occupation. The U.S. government used to call it occupation, and used to reject its measures and reject this and that, and used to call to the implementation of the Geneva agreement. This was the official America, State department and otherwise. It tried to, because all became a United Nations, so you no longer have the right to resist the occupation. All of that will be classified according to the American concept. There is no occupation now. There is an understanding and there are no weapons to be carried because there is no occupation to be fought. There is no more suffering because of the occupation. Suffering now is on the hands of the local government. This will be classified as terrorism according to America. How are you going to do it? How are you going to perform jihad?"

Q. Okay. Agent Burns, have we already heard in some of the calls or some of the segments that we have played or read a discussion for a new organization?

A. Yes.

Q. Has that discussion – did that happen several times where they discussed creating a new organization?

A. It did.

Q. Okay.

MR. JONAS: If we can turn to Philly Meeting No. 5, and the excerpt if we can get page 1 on the screen, please.

Q. (BY MR. JONAS) Agent Burns, I will give your voice a break and I will just read this one. Unknown male 2 says, "In my opinion, we must form a new organization for activism which will be neutral because we are placed in a corner. We are placed in a corner. It is known who we are. We are marked. And I believe that there should be a new neutral organization which works on both sides so that – because this state is coming no matter what, and this is a new existing order." Agent Burns, were there any other discussions about them being marked?

A. Yes.

MR. JONAS: If we can turn to Philly Meeting No. 13 in the excerpt, and if we can play segments F and G, please. (Whereupon, Philly Meeting No. 13-E, Segment F and G were played, while questions were propounded.)

> UM2: Yes, for the Palestinians. If there is an idea to adopt a specific project which earns Muslim people's sympathy in America, it is always the Jerusalem issue.
>
> ... The last issue which needs a quick look is the issue our brother and some of the brothers spoke about is that we could use an official cover such...UI, insurance and stuff. Therefore, I wrote about a point which should be taken into consideration which is making available an official U.S. cover representing the Islamic community in general terms, you see? This way, we can visit Palestine not as Holy Land Foundation because the Holy Land Foundation is stamped already as...er, whatever. So, if we collected a group of representatives of Islamic organizations, one from ISNA, one from ICNA and one from here and there, and formed an official delegation representing the Islamic community in America and announced in a studied format that we will be going to the Occupied Territories and Gaza in particular, you see, to provide assistance to Islamic foundations which are already established [*there*]. This will achieve more than one goal; first, we exhibit the existence of an Islamic concern for the cause even though it is...UI, secondly, we give an official cover for the existing organizations in case they got dissolved or if the [*Palestinian Liberation*] Organization wanted to dissolve these organizations or shut them down, they will take into account that there are some people abroad who show concern about these issues. It also gives a future cover to provide these organizations with money.

Q. (BY MR. JONAS) Do you see where it says ISNA and ICNA? Have we seen those names before?

A. Yes.

Q. Where?

A. ISNA was on several of the documents we have already discussed as one of the Muslim Brotherhood organizations.

> *The Islamic Society of North America (ISNA), was an organization formed out of the Muslim Brotherhood controlled Muslim Students Association beginning in 1977. Muslim Brotherhood documents would describe ISNA as the "Nucleus" of the Islamic Movement in the United States. Following the conclusion of the Holy Land Foundation Trial, Federal Judge Jorge Solis would confirm that the U.S. Government had provided "ample evidence" during trial to connect ISNA with the Holy Land Foundation, Palestine Committee and Hamas. In particular, ISNA bank accounts, through its subsidiary the North American Islamic Trust, shared bank accounts with the Holy Land Foundation.[27] The Islamic Circle of North America (ICNA) was the front organization of the Pakistani Islamist group Jamaat-e-Islami[28], which merged with the U.S. Muslim Brotherhood as noted in the "1991 Explanatory Memorandum."[29]*

...

THE COURT: Mr. Jonas?

MR. JONAS: Thank you, sir.

Q. (BY MR. JONAS) Agent Burns, the last segment we played from Philly Meeting No. 13-E, the unidentified male that was speaking said that the Holy Land Foundation was stamped, or ready as whatever. And the prior segment I read from Philly Meeting No. 5, the unidentified male talked about that "We are placed in a corner. It is known who we are. We are marked." Okay?

MR. JONAS: Per stipulation, Your Honor, I would like to read to the jury, upon agreement of the parties, the following: "As of the date of the Philadelphia meeting, the HLF has been publicly named in a newspaper article as being associated with Hamas."

THE COURT: Okay. And that stipulation the parties have agreed to, so you can accept that as an established fact without hearing any additional evidence. I guess for the record we should get – Mr. Cline, that is language you have agreed to. Correct?

MR. CLINE: Yes, Your Honor.

THE COURT: On behalf of all counsel and all the parties?

MR. CLINE: Yes, Your Honor.

MR. JONAS: Thank you, sir.

Q. (BY MR. JONAS) Agent Burns, that Philly Meeting No. 5 segment I read, as well as some other segments we read and played, discussed a new organization being created. A neutral organization is a term that was used. Do you have before You Elbarasse Search 19?

A. I do.

Q. Okay. And what is the date of that document?

A. July 30th, 1994.

Q. And was this document created – Is that after the Philly Meeting in 1994?

A. It is.

MR. JONAS: Your Honor, at this time I would offer into evidence Elbarasse Search No. 19.

THE COURT: That is admitted.

MR. JONAS: If we could put page 1 of that on the screen, first.

UASR   HLF   IAP

CAIR

Q. (BY MR. JONAS) Agent Burns, what language is this document in?

A. It is primarily in Arabic, but there are a few words there that were in English in the original document.

Q. Starting with the English words on this first page that you see, what are those organizations? What is that?

52

A. The UASR that we have discussed at length, the HLF, the IAP, and a new organization CAIR.

Q. Was this page translated?

A. It was.

Q. The whole document was translated?

A. It was.

MR. JONAS: If we can go to page 6.

Q. (BY MR. JONAS) What is the title of this document?

A. "Meeting agenda for the Palestine Committee, July 30th, 1994."

Q. And if you go to No. 3, can you read what it says?

A. It says, "Reviewing reports of the working organizations, and it includes: "Reviewing work report of the previous stage. "Financial situation. "Future suggestions to develop work of the following organizations: IAP, HLF, UASR, Coordination, CAIR."

Q. Do you know what CAIR stands for?

A. Yes.

Q. What does it stand for?

A. Council on American-Islamic Relations.

Q. Prior to the Philadelphia meeting did you see the organization CAIR mentioned in any of the Elbarasse documents?

A. It did not exist prior to the Philadelphia meeting.

Q. So it came into being after Philadelphia?

A. That is correct.

> *Here Agent Burns and acting District Attorney Jonas confirm that CAIR was an organization created and controlled by the Palestine Committee, with the explicit purpose of fulfilling the concerns raised at 1993 Philadelphia Meeting. This particular section culminates with the identification of CAIR as the new organization that was proposed and discussed throughout the entirety of the Philadelphia Meeting.*

Q. Okay. Were there any additional discussions by the participants about how they would portray themselves to America?

A. Yes.

MR. JONAS: If we turn to Philly Meeting No. 16 and the excerpts, if we can play Segment F and G together, please. (Whereupon, Philly Meeting NO. 16-E, Segment F and G were played, while questions were propounded.)

Q. (BY MR. JONAS) Who is speaking here?

A. This is the Defendant Shukri Abu Baker.

Q. Agent Burns, did you see in that segment where the Defendant Shukri Baker talked about making presentations on human suffering and the rights, the issues he understands, he says?

A. Yes.

Q. Were there additional discussions making presentations to America on human rights?

A. Yes.

MR. JONAS: If we can go to Philly Meeting No. 10, Segment G. That is on page 5 of the excerpted portion. If we can put that on the screen, please, the bottom segment.

Q. (BY MR. JONAS) What does this unidentified male say, please?

A. He says, "The first is to make the agreement fail, and this is a public policy and all of us are opposing it. It is the just the media which exaggerated the issue. Second, finding the alternatives. The first step should be taken advantage of by the brothers in – how to make the agreement fail. The national rights, human rights, stuff which will be exploited in order to make you look legitimate while you call on the annulment of the agreement. I mean, there should be legitimacy to everything we do so that they won't – they should always be in – this is one aspect. The other aspect is working to find the alternatives. Create programs in order to target the agreement."

Q. Agent Burns, were there other discussions about exploiting human rights?

A. Yes.

MR. JONAS: If we can go to Philly Meeting No. 12 and play Segment D. (Whereupon, Philly Meeting NO. 12, Segment D was played, while questions were propounded.)

Q. (BY MR. JONAS) Agent Burns, did you see where the Defendant Shukri Baker talked about neglecting camps in the past?

A. I did.

Q. Did he talk – Were there any other times where he talked about the camps and taking advantage of them?

A. Yes.

MR. JONAS: If we can turn to Philly Meeting No. 14-E for the excerpt, play Segment B, please.

(Whereupon, Philly Meeting No. 14-E, Segment B was played, while questions were propounded.)

Q. (BY MR. JONAS) Agent Burns, some of the words are cut off on the right. Do you see that on your screen?

A. I do.

Q. Do you have this particular portion in your transcript in front of you?

A. I do. It may take me just a minute to find it. Okay. I have it.

Q. Go ahead.

A. Beginning with "Stressing the suffering," "Stressing the suffering in the Palestinians' camps in Palestine and outside it. The camps program which is excluded in the agreement process...the suffering still exists, and we could benefit from the suffering in the camps from the angle of approaching the Palestinian cause from this angle at least. Inside Palestine and in all the camps all over the world. The third item is focusing on the humanitarian needs which are not much affected by the political changes to start with. An example is the orphan sponsorship program. It has no relationship with the changes. Okay? The needy or the handicapped child fund, the student fund, anti-poverty projects, these are projects which will remain even if there is a Palestinian state in place. How much more for people without a leadership? The...always negates the religious sentiment at the donors. There is a religious sentiment at the donor. I tell him, 'Come on. You will give you zakat out anyway. Give me your zakat and I will send it to Palestine.' He will give it anyway. It won't make a difference to him. Sacrifices, establishing endowment projects and drinking fountains and carrying out the legitimate will project. It is a long term plan. That's fine. Now, if three or four people wrote their wills, we could get half a million dollars. It is a long term, but it is a legitimate will which he will carry out whether with you or with somebody else, focusing on the importance of supporting the Islamic organizations in the upcoming stage. I will speak about a specific population which is the Islamic population. See, if we don't support the Islamic organizations, other organizations will come to destroy and crush them. The Islamic University, the University, this is a very private address. I cannot place an ad in the newspaper saying, 'Save the Islamic institutions. 'Starting a dialogue with the American public to contribute to the new phase of rebuilding in Gaza and Jericho. This is an important issue. What happened. Why should I rely on self-rule? No. Come here. I go to the American public and tell him, 'That is excellent. Good. We are going to build Gaza and we are going to build Jericho. I want you to help me.' That is because I will be in a position of competition with the other Palestinian organizations which work with...and which work with the

American public. They will now have impetus, strong media, and they will have strong credibility and legitimacy. We will find ourselves competing with the Americans. Why should I portray myself as...saying that I am an Islamist, only an Islamist, and don't want...don't want the Americans. No, I will open a new dialogue with the Americans and benefit from...and let them go to Jericho and Gaza. Yes, it is not wrong. Seven, start a dialogue with the U.S. and international charitable organizations, U.N organizations, and embarking on new joint projects in Palestine. Please note that if there is one advantage of this Palestinian-Israeli agreement to me, it is that your address to the American public about the Palestinian cause will be easier. The psychological barrier between the Americans and the Palestinian people has begun to erode or disappear. I can benefit from this point by...but I cannot approach them through my strict Islamic address. I can't tell him 'I demand 48 borders.' No way. No way on earth. Okay?"

> *Hamas uses and co-opts non-Islamic charities to accomplish their goals. An excellent example is the recent arrest by Israeli security forces of Gaza project director of the U.S.-based Christian charity World Vision for funneling money to Hamas.*[30] *Additionally,* The United Nations Relief and Works Agency for Palestine Refugees (UNRWA) has repeatedly been credibly accused of being infiltrated by the terrorist group, in a manner strikingly similar to the one described in the Philly Meeting.[31]

Q. Agent Burns, to pause for a moment, what items have we seen that addresses the demanding of 48 borders?

A. Again, that was the Hamas charter.

Q. Okay. Please continue.

A. "No. I approach it through humanitarian suffering, refugees' rights, and issues which the Americans will agree with you on. An example of that is the U.N. organizations and the institutions which give grants, and we could do various projects. Finally, the broad lines which you could call them strategies, one, the...address should steer totally clear from any tension towards the issue of the self-rule. I believe that I as a charity organization should not give an opinion or a political judgment at all. I have no relationship with that. I am not a political institution. I want to...there is a new reality I'm dealing with now. It is not my job to attack the self-rule. This is my view. Amicable relationship must be maintained with all parties inside Palestine. This goes without saying, my brothers. We must not put any factional or partisan influence on the Foundation of America as it is the charitable arm of this or that. No. I say that this is wrong and we must act out of a charitable stand. We must act as an American organization which is registered in America and which cares for the interests of the Palestinian people. It doesn't cater to the interests of a specific party. Our relationship with everyone must be good, regardless." Ghassan Elashi says, "Including the Islamists, of course." And Shukri Abu Baker says, "The Islamists, of course. No, there is no problem, my brother. This is...we gave the Islamists $100,000 and we gave others $5,000."

Q. I believe on the screen it is slightly different, if you could read it.

A. I am sorry. "In the past we gave the Islamists $100,000 and we gave others $5,000."

Q. Agent Burns, is there any other discussion about that last statement, "In the past we gave the Islamists $100,000 and we gave the others $5,000"? Did anyone else reference back to that?

A. Yes.

MR. JONAS: If we can go to Philly Meeting No. 13, segment H, and play that, please.

Q. (BY MR. JONAS) Before we do that, Agent Burns, who are the Islamists, or what are the Islamists as referenced in this case?

A. In this context, the Defendants. That would be people with the Muslim Brotherhood, supporting Hamas, like that.

MS. HOLLANDER: Your Honor, I am going to object to her defining the term Islamist. I don't believe she has any expertise to do that.

THE COURT: Overruled.

Q. (BY MR. JONAS) Who are the others? They say "The Islamists $100,000 and we gave the others $5,000."

A. Anyone else who is not an Islamist.

MR. JONAS: If we can play Segment H of Philly Meeting No. 13. (Whereupon, Philly Meeting No. 13, Segment H was played, while questions were propounded.)

Q. (BY MR. JONAS) Agent Burns, did the Holy Land Foundation give $100,000 to Islamists?

A. They gave much more to Islamists.

Q. As an example, did they give $5,000 or some other nominal amount to others?

A. They did.

Q. Is there a particular of that?

A. One good example that I looked at was a donation to the victims of the Oklahoma City bombing.

Q. Do you have before you what has been marked as InfoCom Search No. 5?

A. I do.

Q. What is that item?

A. It is a thank-you letter from the Oklahoma City Community Foundation to the Holy Land Foundation.

MR. JONAS: Your Honor, at this time I would offer into evidence InfoCom Search No. 5.

MS. HOLLANDER: No objection.

THE COURT: Admitted.

MR. JONAS: If we can put that on the screen, please.

Q. (BY MR. JONAS) What does this document state?

A. It says – Do you want me to read it?

Q. Sure.

A. "On behalf of the citizens of Oklahoma City, Mayor Ronald J. Norick joins me in thanking you for sharing your generosity with the Community Foundation and helping the charitable needs of Oklahoma City. The Oklahoma City Community Foundation thanks you for your gift of $5,000. It will be a credit in your name for the benefit of the Mayor's Disaster Relief Fund."

Q. Agent Burns, were there any phone calls between any of the Defendants regarding the Oklahoma City bombing?

A. Yes.

Q. Who?

A. The Defendants Mohamed El Mezain and Abdulrahman Odeh.

Q. Do you have before you what has been marked as El Mezain Wiretap No. 2?

A. I do.

Q. Is that a phone call?

A. It is.

Q. What is the date of it?

A. April 19th, 1995.

MR. JONAS: Your Honor, at this time I would offer into evidence El Mezain Wiretap No. 2.

THE COURT: Admitted.

MR. JONAS: If we can play that call, please. (Whereupon, El Mezain Wiretap No. 2 was played,while questions were propounded.)

Mo:	Hello.
Ab:	Peace be with you.
Mo:	Peace and God's mercy.
Ab:	How are you, sheik?
Mo:	Good. May God bless you.
Ab:	How are you?
Mo:	May God give you strength.
Ab:	A little while ago, I spoke with Shukri.
Mo:	Hum.
Ab:	So, I don't know... I suggested to him that we must do something regarding this crisis in Oklahoma City.
Mo:	What do you want to do?
Ab:	If they can go there, distribute water to those who work there, send telegrams of condolence to the families of the children who died or stuff, it is a good opportunity, sheik, for us to be highlighted..., that *we do something in America*.
Mo:	Ok, let the...er, let them study the matter from over there.
Ab:	Huh? No, I was just making a suggestion. They are not going to respond to us immediately but,....
Mo:	Let the people....[UI].
Ab:	Because we said in the past in a meeting, my brother, that we must do something in America, or contact the American Red Cross and tell them, "Come, we would like to offer..." because they showed in the news that they are distributing food and water.
Mo:	Yes.
Ab:	So, why can't the *Holy Land* come, for instance, stand and distribute water and stuff.

2

Here Burns and Jonas note how the Palestine Committee used the tragedy of the Oklahoma City bombing in order to raise awareness of their efforts, and to earn public good will. This is a pattern that would be repeated many times over, some with even more sinister effect. In the immediate aftermath of the attacks on 9/11 for example, CAIR would solicit funds on its webpage for the "NY/ DC Emergency Relief Fund." Those who clicked on the link thinking they were providing funds for 9/11 disaster recovery were redirected to the Holy Land Foundation. [32] When this subterfuge was exposed, CAIR instead urged donations directly to the Holy Land Foundation as well as to the Global Relief Fund, another Islamic charity which would be designated by the U.S. Treasury Department for providing funds to Al Qaeda and the Taliban.[33]

Q. (BY MR. JONAS) Who is the MO?

A. That is the Defendant Mohamed El Mezain.

Q. And who is the AB?

A. That is the Defendant Abdulrahman Odeh.

Q. Agent Burns, I want to move away from the Philadelphia meeting.

MR. JONAS: Your Honor, I can keep going, or we can break. It is up to you?

THE COURT: Are you at a good breaking point?

MR. JONAS: Yes.

THE COURT: Let's go ahead and break for the day, then. Be back at 9:00 in the morning. Please recall the instructions about not discussing the case with anyone or not reading anything about it. (Whereupon, the jury left the courtroom.)

APPENDIX I: PHILLY MEETING 2

The Philly Meeting 2 transcript contains two longer presentations, one by an unidentified male speaker, and one by Gawad Al-Awad, of the Palestine Section. The Palestine Section is identified in Muslim Brotherhood archival documents as the Muslim Brotherhood organization of the Sham Countries (meaning Lebanon, Syria and Jordan), responsible for overseeing and coordinating support for the "Movement" inside the territories.[34]

These presentations are followed by a back and forth where Omar Ahmad and Nihad Awad discuss the logistics of founding a new organization in Washington.[35] Ahmad and Awad complain about the need for increased funds. Awad also notes that discussions regarding a new organization, which would become CAIR, began the previous year, well before the Philly Meeting, and refers explicitly to the Palestine Committee, reflecting his direct knowledge of this covert Brotherhood organization.

Ni: Yeah. But, a lot of the things we call long-term suggestions are...UI. If you are going to tell yourself that everything you have is for the long-range, you will keep postponing it. If it is for the long-range you will not work for it from now. These are things you must think about beginning today. Otherwise, when are you going to start thinking about them. I mean, you say that you want to establish an organization in Washington. How long have you been thinking about it? It is not since July. You have been thinking about it over a year ago.

Om: Yes, right.

Ni: It is the same thing for these matters. When you think about the future of activism, it is in two parts; one deals with the current reality and another pertains to what you want to be in the future. You don't...

Om: Yes. But, what I mean that you shouldn't..., that we shouldn't take on the educational role, the awareness role, the role of forming a generation. I mean, we keep telling the community that...UI.

Ni: No. We didn't say that. You're saying that because you were sleeping. What I said is that wherever there are community concentrations... [laughter].

UM2: What are you saying, Omar?

Om: ...UI.

Ni: What I said is that wherever there are gatherings for the Palestinian community..., they are looking for people to teach Arabic to their children. They look for people to teach their children something about culture and heritage. We don't have to open a school for them. Why should I open schools for them. I just tell them "Here is the school", you know. I tell them "Try. Bring your kids". I send someone to them, for instance. That's what I'm saying. I'm not saying that I will open schools and open universities for them. But, if you don't provide services for them, how are you going to bring them over? You're just going to tell them come and visit me?

Om: I believe..., I believe that there is an important step which we must take now. Let's say it clearly, we have 300-400 people from the countries of Syria, Lebanon and Palestine and you don't see 50 people out of them. Where are the 350 people? We need at least 200 people who are sympathetic to the cause and who interact with the news as soon as they hear it. As for those who remain asleep, we alone will not be able to perform these duties. We need those 200 people. We should make a target to get those 200 people to work in the same manner on this cause, for instance. No matter what happens even if the Group gets agitated we must achieve our goals.

Ni: You see, this is not the job of the executive committee for the [*Islamic*] Association [*for Palestine*]. It is the job of the Palestine Committee.

[*UI brief group talk*].

Om: My opinion is that this is the duty of all of us because it is not... Because there are brothers who...UI. They must be convinced. My brothers, we should come to a brother and we tell him "Come here. What is your duty? What do you do?". Each one of us should convince 3, 4 or five people. Each one in his region can influence 3 or 4 people. It is not possible unless we influence 5 or 6 people. If we exert our effort and energy and tried to increase the number of the observant activist..., just to try to increase their number. If we increase their number, we increase our gateway to the communities. If we specify the goal we will be able to spread more. This is a step. The second step is very necessary which is the issue of ...UI. For instance, we spoke about money and stuff. It is important to do even if from our personal investments. We should allocate a sum of money and invest it in order to bring us [*revenue*] for a project. For instance, projects...UI half of which is from us and the other half should go, for instance, to the [*Islamic*] Association [*for Palestine*] or to this activism on which we agree even if it is a small amount; 40,000, 50,000, 100,000 or 70,000 no matter what. We must start because he who starts now will reach the goal in ten years. He who thinks about the [*Islamic*] Association [*for Palestine*] and other things must.... I mean, this [*Islamic*] Association [*for Palestine*] and other things... I will give you an example. When we started Al Zaytouna, we started it with 4 pages and now it is 16 pages. Had we started with 16 pages we would not have been able to finish it within a week. Impossible. Because we were not used to that. Things can happen gradually. Hadn't we started with 4 pages two years ago we wouldn't have reached 16 pages. If we start with a 10,000 investment it will become 100,000, for instance, in five years. But, if we start with a zero and waited for the million to come, neither the million or anything else will come after five years. All of our work must start this way. We must start small and then grow. I believe that there is an influence on us from the Group, a negative influence, as there is a state of laxity and stuff. This has influenced us as we lost hope that this method will work. On the contrary, I believe that it is a strong method and it is also the best one but the circumstances surrounding us are bad. So, you think that this Movement or this thing has stopped to function. Therefore, we must restore its power to it again as it is the origin to restore power to us. Think that we meet some people and we might be seeing them for the first time and we talk honestly and with all confidence. But, if this Group that binds us does not exist you will find one person suspicious of another and God knows where he is from. One person speaks while

APPENDIX II: PHILLY MEETING 4

Philly Meeting 4 contains large sections of frank talk about how the Palestine Committee members view the struggle against Israel, and more broadly, other conflicts where Islamists are opposing secular or non-Muslim governments. An unidentified male refers to Islamists fighting in Algeria, Syria, Egypt, Tunisia and Iraq, noting that the motivating factor is the imposition of Sharia law (quoted in the transcript as "God's Sharia". CAIR founder Omar Ahmad concurs with this, noting that the Palestinians were fighting "The biggest enemy of Islam." This is an important reminder that while CAIR was founded as part of the Palestine Committee for the purpose of supporting Hamas, ultimately broader objectives, i.e. imposing Sharia, remained the ultimate goal not contingent upon nationalist or ethnic struggles.

UM1: So, now the Algerian who is fighting in Algeria, the Egyptian who is fighting in Egypt, the Tunisian who is fighting in Tunisia, the Iraqi in Iraq and the Syrian in Syria and everywhere..., the legal status of their fighting is..., What? What I really want to say is that if we don't focus on the doctrinal and the Sharia issue we are not really presenting any new legitimacy for our work. If I clothe or feed a Palestinian or stuff this will not

silence the people of Islam and the people of faith from pursuing the cause.

Ak: This is what I mentioned at the beginning. Our undisputable rights.

UM1: I mean....,

Ak: I said that at the beginning. Our rights in Palestine don't have anything to do with any living conditions. We have undisputable rights in Palestine as Islamists. They don't change with the changing of the events.

UM1: But, our issue now is..., it is even a fundamental issue that blocking the Sharia of God, fighting Islam and confronting God the Almighty..., this is a grand issue. May it be good, God's willing.

Om: We are confronting the biggest enemy for Islam.

UM1: What?

Om: We in Palestine are confronting the biggest enemy of Islam. It is..., it is a two-sided enemy, an enemy of Islam and an enemy of...UI.

This is followed by Omar Ahmad's presentation. Ahmad weighs in on the issue of cooperating with other Islamic organizations, notably the AMC, the American Muslim Council, founded by Holy Land Foundation unindicted co-conspirator and convicted Al Qaeda fundraiser Adurrahman Alamoudi, and MAS, the Muslim American Society identified by federal prosecutors in a separate trial as the "overt arm" of the Muslim Brotherhood in the United States.

There is a very good reason for that. It is in order to unify the forces...., the position of the Islamic forces in a unified activism program for Palestine. If the positions of the Islamic organizations started to contradict, which is what is currently happening as the [Islamic] Association [for Palestine] is saying one thing, the AMC is saying one thing, MAS is saying another thing and they say that the Pakistanis are talking about moon sighting and everyone is saying something different, when there is such a contradiction in the positions of the different Islamic organizations it will weaken the Islamic position in regards to Palestine a great deal. Then we as the [Islamic] Association [for Palestine], as people who are responsible for Islamic activism for Palestine that there is a state of great weakness and acute frailty in our position because we then...UI our position with Muslims. Therefore, we must be careful that the positions of Muslims remain the same. This unified program should mobilize Muslims for the Islamic project through the unity of logic and direction. If the thinking of Muslims is unified with you their mobilization will be easy. You tell them "Coordinate with me. All of Palestine is for Muslims. You coordinate with me that our position regarding Gaza-Jericho is so and so. How about you and me hold this seminar, this conference, this donation". This can be done through notifying the organizations of our position in a continuous and clear manner and establishing official and personal with them and giving them a role in determining the Islamic position in regards to Palestine and the appropriate method of address in America. This is the outcome of experience. You must first tell them what is our position. It is not enough that we wait for someone to call us and ask us "By God, what is your position in the issue", or wait for us. No, we go to him, make the initiative and tell him "Our position is like that; one, two, three, four". And we should make sure, make sure that he got the message and understands it so that when he stands up to talk he wouldn't say stuff we didn't mean by our statements. There should also be personal and official relationships between us and them. This means that we should a personal relationship between us and the guy who is in charge of that organization. And also an official relationship in our capacity as the [Islamic] Association [for Palestine], we should have mutual positions where we supported him in positions. This is America all over; organizations with interests. They should also be partners in determining the Islamic position for Palestine. It is not enough that we say "By God, my position is so and so. Go ahead, adopt this position and go on". You must make him a partner in the decision, present to him and discuss it. You then stay with them to write the final wording of the position. And I believe that this work must be done. This might not be a fast way to do it but, in the future, there could be certain mechanism to unify the Islamic position in all of America. As for the organizations which want to dissent from the Islamic position for personal interests or out of fear... I mean, there are Islamic organizations such as the AMC and others which want to dissent from the Islamic position, either for personal interests, to promote itself, or for fear. We must pressure them and embarrass them by various means until they adhere to our position or, at least, remain neutral. This is something...., Maher

Ahmad also mentions discussing issues with Maher Hathout, the founder of the Islamic Shura Council of Southern California and the Muslim Public Affairs Council (MPAC). Ahmad goes on to name MPAC explicitly.[36] Ahmad also suggests a wider political activism on Islamic issues in order to conceal and whitewash efforts aimed at support for Islamists, a tactic clearly adopted by CAIR in the years that followed the Philly Meeting.

Hathout said that thing when we were at the...UI. He said "If the Palestinians say this and that we are with them". If the Palestinians abandoned Palestine you must speak up as an Islamist. He said "But you Palestinians say this and that and there are pressures on us and stuff". I told him "If you are under pressure then stay silent. You don't have to say yes or no. Just stay silent and remain neutral". We shouldn't let these people....., these people splinter the unity of the Islamic Palestinian front. Thus, we should pressure them by various means until they either adhere to our position or remain neutral. Also, forming a lobby for the decision-makers abroad. This is also a very important thing. It is a long-term goal. This can be achieved through our popular, political, financial and media strength in America. I mean, when we are strong like I said in the beginning, I can be a means for pressure on them but if we are weak and we don't have an Islamic community, we don't have influence over the Congress or the organizations such as the ADC, ...UI and others people won't pay attention to us. This will also bolster our position in America with the U.S. Administration and other media and political organizations. If we are strong we can influence what they decide over there, for instance. If Yasser Arafat were to think twice before he does something in America because he worries about the Islamic community in America it would give us some sort of credit with the U.S. Administration or media outlets....UI in addition to the fact that it reinforces the position of the pro-Islamic solution for Palestine abroad and lessens the danger those who surrendered. When we are strong, people who are against surrender will see that they have a large community in America which supports them financially and stands with them. It pressures the other people which reinforces their position. This is the thing..., the thing brother Gawad spoke about. He said that it won't be achieved unless we are strong in this country. The other thing is in regards to political activism is lessening the animosity of America and the West to Muslims and to Palestinians, in particular because pressure now is not only on Muslims but they focus on the term Palestinian-Islamic such as Mohamed Salam and others. I mean they focus on the fact that this guy is Palestinian and an Islamist because the Jews' target is the Palestinian individual. Also, strengthening the influence with Congress or other than the Congress. This is also one of the long-term goals but we have started to do some things about it. This can be achieved by infiltrating the American media outlets, universities and research centers as we previously said. It is also achieved by working with Islamic political organizations and the sympathetic ones such as..., you have now many emerging Islamic organizations, such as the American Muslim Alliance, such as the United Muslims of America, MPAC and AIPAC and others. All of those try to...UI and recruit Muslims to engage in political activism in America and I think that it is our mission to assist them because if Muslims engage in political activism in America and started to be concerned with Congress and public relations we will have an entry point to use them to pressure Congress and the decision-makers in America.

****

Page 17 of 18

17

68

Appendix III: Philly Meeting 7

In addition to referencing 1993 World Trade Center bombing conspirator Omar Abdel Rahman, in this transcript Omar Ahmad describes the struggle involved with the formation of a new organization (that will become CAIR).

Ahmad notes that while establishing new organizations is a simple task, the struggle faced by the Palestine Committee is the lack of available supporters with which to fill the positions.

Om: Someone will do that. So, you will be in a problem. But, legally, I see that we don't have any..., I mean I'm personally comfortable that we don't have a problem with the law if we covered these two things.

UM1: Ok, the other point is: Is it wrong if we wanted to form an organization from a precautionary point of view? I mean, just in case...

Om: Let me tell you...

UM1: ...just in case something happened to the [*Islamic*] Association [*for Palestine*], God forbid. And I'm not saying it will be a...UI organization. No, we will give the same input. We will not change as it is a matter of principle.

Om: [*You mean*] as a quick alternative.

UM1: But, suppose they cornered us regarding this point we would have another way out. Is this wrong to think about?

Om: No, it is not. But, where is the problem? It is that there are no available people to work. I mean, you say...

UM1: Let it get registered and....

Om: ...UI. Registering an organization is easy. I can register 100 organizations in 100 cities in one day. Registration is not important. Here in America you begin working first and then you then go register. It is not a problem here.

UM1: Yes.

Page 5 of 20

Ahmad notes, "Like I told you, go-ahead start a new organization but you won't be able to find new faces. Do we have hidden faces we now bring up to light? We have what we have. I mean, we don't really have available people whom we could dedicate for the work we want to hide."

Om: The problem is where? We don't have available people to work in the existing organization. Where do we go to find these people? Like I told you, go ahead start a new organization but you won't be able to find new faces. Do we have hidden faces we now bring up to light? We have what we have. I mean, we don't really have available people whom we could dedicate for the work we want to hide. We don't have available people to work right now. This is one. The idea which we can discuss in more details is whether we should drop our Islamic identity or keep it.

UM1: Yes.

UM2: Let us discuss this point after we listen to brother Nihad regarding the issue of political and media address and how it should be for the American people for members of the Islamic and Arabic community, and how do we handle our issues with the brothers.

UM1: I just have a remark.

UM2: Hum. Go ahead.

UM1: The idea behind the goal which was discussed is meant to stir discussion around it and not for..., by God... First of all, I don't adopt it as an idea but as an idea to be discussed on the table. Every brother is supposed to give his ideas around it and not block it.

UM2: You mean tweak it.

UM1: I mean all the ideas which were suggested to destroy this goal. But, suggesting a goal like that and points like these are meant for discussion to see if this thing is applicable, can this thing benefit us in the future. We now jump to conclusions so fast. Our inclination might not be to go mingle with people, drink and dance and stuff like that. The idea..., the idea is to create an organization and we need to discuss it in a scientific manner and not in a discussion in which we jump into conclusions. I'm not going to keep defending it...

This reality mentioned by Ahmad would be a sticking point for CAIR, law enforcement and outside counterterrorism researchers would again and again note the recurrence of CAIR staff linked to Palestine Committee organizations, such as the Holy Land Foundation, Islamic Association of Palestine, or United Association for Studies and Research.

APPENDIX IV: PHILLY MEETING 12

Philly Meeting 12 begins with back and forth over whether the assembled members should vote on the decision to expand the scope of the Islamic Association for Palestine (IAP)'s work into media issues. During the discussion Omar Ahamd warns Abdel Halim Al Ashqar (identified as As:)

"When there is ... , there is a media situation and a situation where the FBI comes to you at your house so that half of the people don't attend your festival and tell you, "I'm afraid to attend your festival because there is talk about you". This is the talk. Give me two years while the situation remains like that and the Jews will come and ... Tomorrow, the Jews will use the media [and say], "The Islamic Association for Palestine and stuff. It does this and that". Not a single person will go to the festival."

Om: When there is..., there is a media situation and a situation where the FBI comes to you at your house so that half of the people don't attend your festival and tell you, "I'm afraid to attend your festival because there is talk about you". This is the talk. Give me two years while the situation remains like that and the Jews will come and... Tomorrow, the Jews will use the media [*and say*], "The Islamic Association for Palestine and stuff. It does this and that". Not a single person will go to the festival.

UM2:   Then, specify..., specify your points. Don't go around saying...UI in the community.

Om: I'm specifying points...

Sh: Be patient, our brothers. Let's finish. We're now in a position to specify points or cite examples...UI.

Om: My brother, just a minute. Today in Philadelphia... Yesterday, in the festival, the tickets sold were more than those who attended. Usually, when we sell tickets, double the number attend. Why? People tell you, "I will purchase a ticket but I don't want to come". This is what people say "I will purchase. I'm ready to give you the $10, but I don't want to come. I don't want to attend with you". What is this catastrophe? Half of the people didn't attend because of that reason. They're afraid. They tell you, "You're..., you're scary. Let me..., I will give you". Someone said, "I will give you $1,000 cash.

In fact CAIR would indeed serve to defend those investigated by the FBI for terrorism ties, including Al-Ashqar, just as Ahmad had warned. When Ashqar was incarcerated for contempt after refusing to testify before a grand jury, CAIR wrote a letter to the judge in support of Ashqar's "positive contributions to this society." Numerous other examples of CAIR defending terror suspects are notable, including convicted Palestinian Islamic Jihad leader Sami Al-Arian.[37]

APPENDIX V: PHILLY MEETING 16

In Philly Meeting 16, Nihad Awad is presenting about media aspects of the Palestine Committee's work. In particular he discusses the nature of how to present their position in support of Hamas and in opposition to the peace agreement. This leads to a conversation, primarily between Nihad Awad and Omar Ahmad, with others chiming in as well, regarding how best to influence other Islamist organizations (which had an American, rather than a Palestinian focus) to present the Hamas-approved case for Palestine.

Ni: No. Stay with me. My brother, I see another thing. Did you see the programs which were aired after the signing and the interviews with the people, the children who are born here, who are non-observant, their statements sounded radical. People seek glory. Those who are scared are the leaders and let's not name names.

UM1: Regardless....UI.

Om: We don't want leaders other than the existing ones. They signed the statement.

Ni: And that's why they signed the statement. That's why we modified the language a bit. Unfortunately, people even...UI that our private language which we adopt and which we bear responsibility for is strong and clear.

UM1: If this tells you something, it tells you that the problem is..., the problem is not in the language of the address, not in media. Media is a tool to..., a tool to pass along what you have. The problem really is whether we reached a level of strength whereby we tell the Islamic organizations "This is the position of Islam in Palestine. Are you going to adhere to it or else...?". We didn't reach this stage. When we reach this stage the language of the address will be..., they will be looking for a way to manage his situation with.

te

Sh: What do you mean "...or else?". Are you going to close his center for him?

UM1: No. I won't close his center but you can use means..., legal means, legal means and legal reasons to use against him and tell him "Your position is either Islamic or non-Islamic. One or the other". As for the language of the address, everyone will tell you "By God, I'm scared of this guy. This guy is my neighbor and this guy is watching me".

UM2: You mean that they don't have an opinion in this issue, the Islamic organizations? I tell you, this is what I noticed, all the Islamic organizations such as ISNA, ICNA and others wish to see the day you issue a statement in your name and that's it. You are a specialized entity and you leave them alone.

The topic drifts into how best to hold Islamic organizations accountable to Islamic jurisprudence related to the conflict, with Unidentified Male # noting,

"Therefore, when I read these things, these are [sic] legal matters, people will have ... ul. You see? So, we are trying to ignore the legal position in matters in favor for political hues. This is what is ruining things."

74

CAIR founder Omar Ahmad responds by saying, "But, you still cannot show the legal position to the Americans..."

The meeting participants are than recorded laughing as Unidentified Male #1 notes that he will not "be naïve enough to tell the Americans, "it is my right to enslave your daughter," or to repeat 1993 World Trade Center mastermind Omar Abdel Rahman statement that "America is plunder for us" even while he agrees "his words are correct." CAIR executive Director Nihad Awad also weighs in, in support of Islamic law.

Om: But, you still cannot show the legal position to the Americans...UI

UM1: No, my brother. There are things I can warn against such as... I won't be naive to the point of telling the American "It is my right to enslave your daughter and...", like what Omar Abdel Rahman did in Detroit and said that "America will be a plunder for us". His words are correct [*Laughter and UI brief group comments*]. No, really. It was wrong.

Ni: By God, by God, I don't see any embarrassment in speaking about Islamic Sharia because it is...UI. If we can make people...UI it should be convincing. If we don't like it., UI

UM1: Is this your faith in God and your faith in Islam?

UM2: Even some of..., some of the members of the [*Palestinian Liberation*] Organization when they used to rush to U.S. TV, before the peace treaty issue was presented and stuff like that, when they were opposed to it..., I remember Hatem Hussein in the beginning of 80's and stuff, he used to say "We want our share in it. We want El Lod, Ramallah and stuff like that". And they used to cite examples saying "If someone comes to your house and stole something. Would you accept that or not?". The Americans used to hear this kind of talk. They liked it or not..., but the input was similar. So, the Americans..., we must address them from a position of right and justice and, at the same time, choose our words well. I mean we shouldn't mess up like Omar Abdel Rahman and fight and stuff like that. The guy who opposes the treaty, Netanyahu, found a way to address the American public opinion. They accept him, that's true, because he is an Israeli and like him more than us, of course, he is Jewish, you see? But, he found a path that is different from Rabin's, you see? He stressed his convictions in Palestine and stuff like that and rejected the treaty and told them "I would like peace also but, people in Palestine will do this and that". Stuff like that. We could also...UI.

These statements are a reminder that while CAIR is aggressively engaged in opposing efforts to inform Americans about the nature of Sharia law and its incompatibility with the American constitutional system ultimately CAIR's founders, and the Muslim Brotherhood network more broadly, continued to quietly support it.

Notes

[1] "Exhibit Elbarasse Search-5" *United States v. Holy Land Foundation for Relief and Development (HLF) et.al*, accessible at http://coop.txnd.uscourts.gov/judges/hlf2/09-25-08/Elbarasse%20Search%205.pdf

[2] "Interview under Proffer Agreement 1/06/05" *Federal Bureau of Investigation*, (January 6, 2005), accessible at: http://www.investigativeproject.org/documents/misc/847.pdf

[3] "Philly Meeting 15-E", *United States v. HLF et al.*, accessible at: http://coop.txnd.uscourts.gov/judges/hlf2/09-29-08/Philly%20Meeting%2015E.pdf

[4] "House Resolution No. 170" *Louisiana House of Representatives*, (2016), http://www.legis.la.gov/legis/ViewDocument.aspx?d=1004598

[5] Levitt, Matthew, "Prosecuting Terrorism Supporters: Lessons from a Recent Verdict," Washington Institute, (February 2007), http://www.washingtoninstitute.org/policy-analysis/view/prosecuting-terrorism-supporters-lessons-from-a-recent-verdict and Investigative Project on Terrorism, "Ashqar Gets 11 Years for Contempt," (November 21, 2007), http://www.investigativeproject.org/554/ashqar-gets-11-years-for-contempt#

[6] For Ahmad's ties to Islamic Association of Palestine see: Nihad Awad, "Muslim Americans in Mainstream America," *The Link* (February-March 2000), https://web.archive.org/web/20030615211502/http://www.ameu.org/uploads/vol33_issue1_2000.pdf

[7] Richard C. Powers, "Letter to the Honorable John Kyl," U.S. Department of Justice, (April 28, 2008), accessible at: http://www.investigativeproject.org/documents/misc/265.pdf

[8] Scott Gordon, "Dallas Islamic Leader Deported," NBC 5 News, February 19, 2010, http://www.nbcdfw.com/news/local/Dallas-Islamic-Leader-Deported-84809767.html

[9] "Declaration of Special Agent [Redacted]," United States Department of Justice Executive Office for Immigration Review Office of the Immigration Court, (N.D) Dallas, Texas, accessible at: http://www.investigativeproject.org/documents/misc/846.pdf

[10] Department of Justice, "Federal Judge Hands Downs Sentences in Holy Land Foundation Case: Holy Land Foundation and Leaders Convicted on Providing Material Support to Hamas Terrorist Organization" May 27, 2009, https://www.justice.gov/opa/pr/federal-judge-hands-downs-sentences-holy-land-foundation-case

[11] "Government Trial Brief," United States v. Holy Land Foundation et. al., (N.D.), http://www.investigativeproject.org/documents/case_docs/422.pdf page 10

[12] Kyle Shideler "Don Lemon is Wrong About CAIR," Townhall.com (December 11, 2015), http://townhall.com/columnists/kyleshideler/2015/12/11/don-lemon-is-wrong-about-cair-n2092178

[13] Investigative Project on Terrorism, "Islamic Center of Passaic County: Paterson, NJ," *Investigative Project on Terrorism* (N.D.), http://www.investigativeproject.org/mosques/402/islamic-center-of-passaic-county

[14] Kyle Shideler, "Major U.S. Muslim Brotherhood Leader Mohammed Al-Hanooti Dies," Center for Security Policy (June 5, 2015), http://www.centerforsecuritypolicy.org/2015/06/05/major-u-s-muslim-brotherhood-leader-mohammed-al-hanooti-dies/

[15] "Affidavit in support of Search Warrant in the Matter of 4502 Whistler Court, Annandale, VA" United States District Court, Eastern District of Virginia, (August 31, 2004), accessed at http://www.investigativeproject.org/documents/case_docs/1525.pdf

[16] Richard C. Powers, "Letter to the Honorable John Kyl," U.S. Department of Justice, (April 28, 2008), accessible at: http://www.investigativeproject.org/documents/misc/265.pdf

[17] "Council on American Islamic Relations: Links to The United Association for Studies and Research," (July 15, 2010), Anti-Defamation League, http://archive.adl.org/israel/cair/links3.html

[18] Center for Security Policy, "Ikhwan In America: An Oral History of the Muslim Brotherhood in its Own Words" Center for Security Policy Press (April, 27,2016), http://www.centerforsecuritypolicy.org/wp-content/uploads/2016/04/Ikhwan_in_America_20160418.pdf

[19] "Interview under Proffer Agreement 1/06/05" *Federal Bureau of Investigation*, (January 6, 2005), accessible at: http://www.investigativeproject.org/documents/misc/847.pdf

[20] "An Explanatory Memorandum: From the Archives of the Muslim Brotherhood in America," Center for Security Policy Press (2013) http://www.centerforsecuritypolicy.org/wp-content/uploads/2014/05/Explanatory_Memoradum.pdf

[21] Richard Perez-Pena, "THE TERROR CONSPIRACY: THE CHARGES;A Gamble Pays Off as the Prosecution Uses an Obscure 19th-Century Law," New York Times, (October 2, 1995) http://www.nytimes.com/1995/10/02/nyregion/terror-conspiracy-charges-gamble-pays-off-prosecution-uses-obscure-19th-century.html

[22] "Who We Are" CAIR California Website (December 7, 2001), accessed at: https://web.archive.org/web/20011207190546/http://www.cair-california.org/who.htm#Management%20&%20Staff

[23] Sahih Bukhari Hadith 4:269. "Narrated Jabir bin 'Abdullah: The Prophet said, 'War is deceit.'"

[24] "Donor-Affiliated Organization: Council on American Islamic Relations," Islamist Money Watch, (N.D.) http://www.islamist-watch.org/money-politics/donor/352/

[25] See by way of example, "CAIR Reps Visit 113 Congressional Offices," CAIR.com (March, 8, 2012), http://cairunmasked.org/wp-content/uploads/2012/04/CAIR-Reps-visit-113-Congressional-Offices.pdf

[26] IPT News, "Awlaki's U.S. Sermons Foreshadow Role as Terrorist Mentor," Investigative Project on Terrorism, (July 26, 2010), http://www.investigativeproject.org/2077/awlakis-us-sermons-foreshadow-role-as-terrorist

[27] "Memorandum Opinion Order," USA v. Holy Land Foundation for Relief and Development, http://www.investigativeproject.org/documents/case_docs/1425.pdf

[28] See: ICNA's Message International, "Beyond Malcom," (October 1996), saved as a screenshot image and available at: http://www.americansagainsthate.org/Beyond_Malcolm.html
Global Muslim Brotherhood Daily Watch, "Jamaat-e-Islami", (January 17, 2015), http://www.globalmbwatch.com/wiki/jamaat-e-islami/

[29] "An Explanatory Memorandum: From the Archives of the Muslim Brotherhood in America," Center for Security Policy Press (2013) http://www.centerforsecuritypolicy.org/wp-content/uploads/2014/05/Explanatory_Memoradum.pdf

[30] F. Brinley Bruton and Lawahez Jabari, "World Vision's Gaza Manager Funneled Millions to Hamas: Israel," (August 15, 2016) http://www.nbcnews.com/news/world/world-vision-s-gaza-manager-funneled-millions-hamas-israel-n623421

[31] See for example: David Bedein, "Is the US Complicit in UNRWA-Hamas Cooperation?" Algemeiner.com (August 17, 2016), https://www.algemeiner.com/2016/08/17/is-the-us-complicit-in-unrwa-hamas-cooperation/, "UNRWA Official Spoke at Event for Hamas-Linked Charity", The Tower.org (October 24, 2014) http://www.thetower.org/2496-unrwa-official-spoke-at-event-for-hamas-linked-charity/ and
Shawn McCarthy, "Ottawa eyes fresh funding for UN group with alleged ties to Hamas," (February 14, 2016), http://www.theglobeandmail.com/news/politics/ottawa-eyes-fresh-funding-for-un-group-with-alleged-ties-to-hamas/article28757982/

[32] "CAIR National website, September 17, 2001" Screenshot of CAIR Website archived by *Americans Against Hate*, *http://www.americansagainsthate.org/cw/hlf&grf_cw.htm*

[33] Press Release, "Treasury Department Statement Regarding the Designation of the Global Relief Foundation", Treasury Department (October 18, 2002), https://www.treasury.gov/press-center/press-releases/Pages/po3553.aspx

[34] Elbarasse Search-5, "*Islamic Action for Palestine-An Internal Memo*" (October 1992) accessed: http://coop.txnd.uscourts.gov/judges/hlf2/09-25-08/Elbarasse%20Search%205.pdf

[35] Throughout the transcripts Nihad Awad is identified as "Nihad LNU (Last Name Unknown). While he is not identified in the transcripts themselves, the FBI identified Nihad Awad as being present at the Philadelphia Meeting, and Agent Burns testified that Nihad LNU was in fact Nihad Awad of CAIR. For a complete explication on the evidence confirming Nihad Awad's presence at the Philly Meeting see: Investigative Project, "CAIR Executive Director Placed at HAMAS Meeting," *Investigativeproject.com* (August 2, 2007) http://www.investigativeproject.org/282/cair-executive-director-placed-at-hamas-meeting

[36] For more on the Hathout brothers and their association with the Muslim Brotherhood see: The Investigative Project, "Behind the Façade: The Muslim Public Affairs Council" *InvestigativeProject.com* (N.D) http://www.investigativeproject.org/documents/misc/358.pdf

[37] Investigative Project on Terrorism, "CAIR and Terrorism: Blanket Opposition to U.S. Investigations, Equivocal Condemnations for Plots Against America," *Investigativeproject.com (n.d)* http://www.investigativeproject.org/documents/misc/116.pdf

Made in the USA
Las Vegas, NV
13 October 2023

79033424R00052